NEW YORK FAIRIES

A History of the Little People of the Empire State

ANDREW WARBURTON

THE History PRESS

Published by The History Press
An imprint of Arcadia Publishing
Charleston, SC
www.historypress.com

First published 2025
Updated 2026

Manufactured in the United States

ISBN 9781467159739

Library of Congress Control Number: 2025935713

For John

CONTENTS

ACKNOWLEDGEMENTS

I'd like to thank writers who've drawn attention to New York legends about fairies and Little People, including Mason Winfield; James Parker; Mike Adamovic; Camilla Townsend and Nicky Kay Michael; Simon Young and Chris Woodyard; Rob Stephenson; Mitch Waxman; Bob Singleton; and Edward Wozniak. I'd also like to thank those who've communicated with me in person or in writing, including Priscilla Edwards for her knowledge of Bill Greenfield; authors Morgan Daimler and Shaun Cooper for suggesting sources; Mark Hetherington for pointing out the analogous role of imps and fairies in Scottish and English witch trials; Tom Trujillo for his permission to use a Bill Greenfield sketch; Jean Hennessy for her knowledge of the Sacandaga Valley; Nathan Sowry, reference archivist at the National Museum of the American Indian; Reem Kattan for locating Dutch sources; the librarians at Cranston Public Library; the Skä•noñh Great Law of Peace Center in Syracuse; and William Sauers at the Greece Historical Society for access to William Connolly's diary. I'd also like to thank Michael Kinsella for believing in this project and Hilary Parrish for her excellent editing; my friend Sam Baltrusis for showing me the way as an author; Dr. Mary Hemmings for her excellent reading and editing skills and for traveling with me to many of the sites in this book; and John Grillo for his constant support. Lastly, I'd like to thank the readers I've met who believe in fairies, both literal and figurative.

INTRODUCTION

In their book *Other Council Fires Were Here Before Ours* (1991), New Age writer Twylah Nitsch and her granddaughter Jamie Sams mention three different types of Little People who've inhabited the New York region since time immemorial. These Little People include the two-legged type that resemble miniature human beings, the winged type (about which we'll learn more later) and a sparkling type that "appear as shining lights in the dense forest."

In this book, we'll meet many examples of the two-legged type of Little People, drawn from Indigenous and non-Indigenous folklore. We'll also meet the shining-light type, although these appear mainly in Irish American stories and in the findings of the Fairy Census (an online survey of fairy encounters conducted between 2014 and 2023). As for the winged type, very few sightings of winged fairies have been recorded in traditional New York folklore, but they do appear in modern fairy encounters, where we'll meet them in abundance.

Besides these three, we'll also meet fairies that float in the air, live underground and live in water. Whether called fairies or something else like *goblin* or *imp*, all are a type of magical humanoid that, for the purpose of this book, I'll call fairies. Here you'll find stories about beings explicitly known as *fairies* as well as stories about elves, gnomes, will-o'-the-wisps and other enchanting beings.

Wherever you live in New York State, the chances are that the magical events of some fairy story have taken place quite close to you. That's because fairies, whether Little People, banshees or doleful gnomes, can be found in every part of this state—from the Catskills in the south to the Adirondacks in the north, from Fort Niagara in the west to New York City in the east.

Regarding the fairy habitats covered in this book, I include stories from throughout the state, including Upstate New York and New York City, and I cross the state line only once to introduce the fairies of Paterson, New Jersey (a suburb of New York City). Hence, the fairy habitats visited here include the deep forest, remote bodies of water (especially waterfalls) and the bustling metropolis. While the latter may not be where you'd expect to find a fairy, the truth is that fairy folklore has penetrated even into the dense urban jungles of Manhattan, Brooklyn and Queens.

As for the different fairy traditions found in New York, I've divided the material into four separate bodies of folklore. Each is given a dedicated section of this book. These are: Irish American traditions, Dutch-inspired traditions, Indigenous traditions and modern and miscellaneous traditions. I'll introduce them briefly here.

EUROPEAN IMMIGRANT FAIRIES

New York fairy folklorist and storyteller Mabel Powers once claimed that "American children have no fairies of their own." They "must borrow their fairies," she said sadly, "from children of other nations."

In this, Powers was most likely thinking of American children of British descent whose ancestors came here during the country's earliest years, often from places in England where people had ceased to believe in fairies. These "naturalized" children inherited few folkloric ideas about fairies and were raised instead on literary fairy tales and children's books. (Powers must surely have had herself in mind also, for she was a New Yorker of Yankee stock raised very similarly to those "fairy-lacking" children.)

Powers's statement was primarily a poetic observation about "mainstream" America's lack of a national fairy lore. But in 1917, when Powers expressed the sentiment, it wasn't entirely true to say that *no* American children had "fairies of their own."

Between 1852 and 1914, millions of Irish immigrants had come to the United States, many settling in northeastern mill towns like Albany and Troy, New York, and Paterson, New Jersey. No less "American" than the children of earlier immigrants, these newcomers cultivated many folkloric

John Dickson Batten's depiction of one of the Irish Little People, as found in Joseph Jacobs's *More Celtic Fairy Tales* (1895). *Public domain.*

ideas about fairies and passed them on to their children and grandchildren. As a result, a great deal of Irish American fairy lore remained vibrant in New York well into the twentieth century. I introduce these stories in chapter 1 of this book, "Irish Fairies," where I draw on the experiences of Irish Americans from every corner of the state.

The children of Irish immigrants aren't the only residents of the New York region who've had "fairies of their own." Long before the Irish set foot in New York, an entire civilization—which we now call "Dutch America"—arose in Manhattan and along the Hudson River. This occurred in the seventeenth century when the Dutch and British battled for control of the New York region. It's likely that the children of these early settlers remembered stories of goblins and gnomes taught to them in the Netherlands. However, no real firsthand accounts of these stories have survived.

That being said, Dutch folklore entered the American psyche early in the nation's history through the non-Dutch short stories of Washington Irving (1783–1869). Irving was an influential writer of supernatural and not-so-supernatural tales who drew on Dutch traditions in works like "The Storm-Ship" and "Rip Van Winkle." A testament to the power of his stories is that historians and folklorists often came to regard them as more or less faithful renditions of New York folklore. The truth, of course, is more complicated.

WASHINGTON IRVING'S INFLUENCE

Washington Irving is undoubtedly the single most influential figure in the development of New York's non-Indigenous fairy lore. He was one of many nineteenth-century writers who felt that America lacked a national

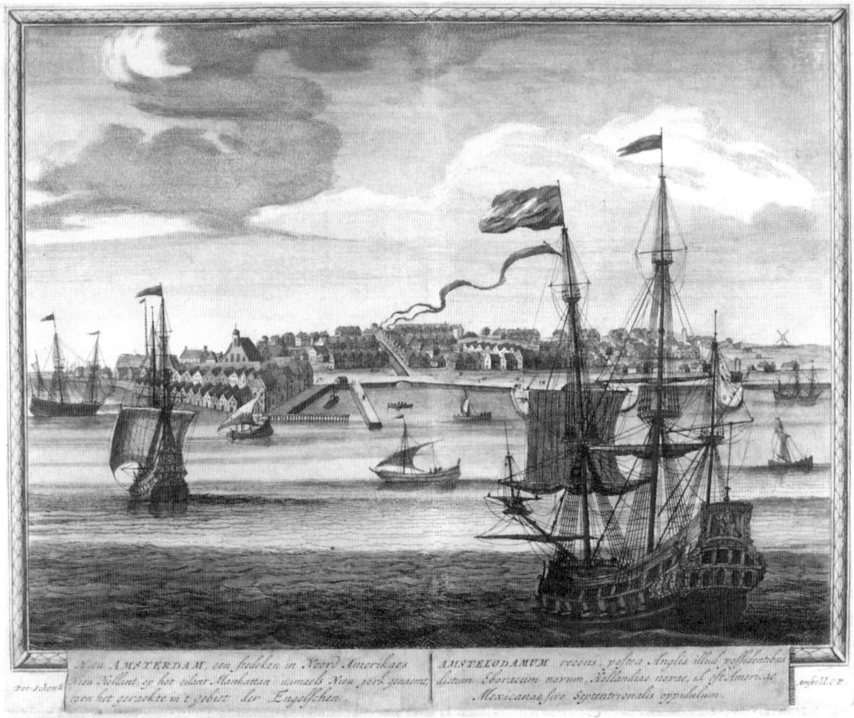

Above: Sketch of New Amsterdam as it appeared in 1673, printed in Peter Schenk's *Hecatompolis* (1702). *Public domain.*

Opposite: Lithograph portrait of Washington Irving made in 1900. *Library of Congress.*

tradition of fairy folklore and who looked with nostalgia at the fairy legends of European nations.

In Europe, the fairies had played an important role not only in the life of the common folk but also in the literature of the land, appearing, for example, in works of genius such as Shakespeare's *A Midsummer Night's Dream*. Irving thought America ought to have an equivalent mythology that would stir the imaginations of its people, and so he set about writing works of mystery imbued with folkloric elements. The results can be seen in famous stories such as "Rip Van Winkle" and "The Legend of Sleepy Hollow."

Based on tidbits of Dutch mythology—often about goblins and gnomes—these stories later became fixtures of the American national consciousness, with folklorists repeating them as if they were records of preexisting legends. Meanwhile, the service industry in New York State, looking to attract tourists to countless newly opened hotels in the countryside, began to associate

Irving's stories with precise locations in New York, including the entrance to the Hudson Highlands (where a goblin king resided on Dunderberg Mountain) and the now-demolished New Grand Hotel in the Catskills (where gnomes consorted once every twenty years). All these developments resulted in a type of newfangled New York fairy lore, largely indebted to the success of the railroad in spreading tourists throughout the state, many of whom adored Irving's works and wished to catch a glimpse of the fairy-haunted landscapes he described.

I introduce Irving's Dutch-flavored tales, specifically "The Storm-Ship" and "Rip Van Winkle," in chapter 2 of this book. I also chart the process by which writers such as Charles Skinner interpreted the goblins and gnomes in these stories as figures of authentic New York folklore.

INDIGENOUS TRADITIONS

Considering what we know about the borrowed nature of many American fairy traditions, we might agree with another of Mabel Powers's statements: that "the only true American fairies" are the Little People of America's Indigenous peoples.

Little People stories are found among the Indigenous nations of the whole of North America. In the United States, Little People folklore stretches from California to New England, from the Great Plains to the Northwest coast. The New York region is no exception, being among the most fertile territories in the nation for Indigenous stories about Little People. In this book, we'll primarily be concerned with stories of the Haudenosaunee Confederacy (often called the Iroquois), a group of six nations based in New York, Canada and the Great Lakes region. We'll also learn about the wood-dwarf and "Doll Spirit" folklore of the Lenape people who once inhabited Manhattan.

One fact that becomes apparent when reading Indigenous folktales about the Little People is that the latter are often noticeably friendlier than the beings of Dutch and Irish lore. Whereas fairies are often dangerous and

Depiction of the Haudenosaunee Little People from Mabel Powers's *Stories the Iroquois Tell Their Children* (1917). *Public domain.*

goblins can be threatening, Indigenous Little People are far more likely to be helpful when they come upon a human.

One example of their kindness comes to us from 1919, when an Oneidan woman called Lydia Doxtater shared a tale about a woman who encountered the Little People while stranded on a lonely island. One night, the woman (who'd built a hut out of hemlock bark) saw many pairs of hands protruding through the door. The hands were extremely chapped, and the woman, surprisingly nonplussed, thought it best to rub them with grease she'd harvested from some game. Soon after that, a group of Little People entered the woman's hut and told her that because she'd cared for their damaged hands, from then on they would bring her the choicest foods and entertain her with singing and dancing. As promised, they did this every night until the woman's people finally came and rescued her from the island.

Another important aspect of Indigenous New York folklore is the sacred ceremonial significance the Little People hold for some Indigenous people. Members of the Seneca Nation have long propitiated the Little People with tobacco while performing a ritual called the Dark Dance (more on that later). As for the Lenape people, their folklore suggests that wood dwarves and Doll Spirits once played an important role in the spiritual lives of the people.

Indigenous folklore about the Little People can be found in chapter 3 of this book. All the stories in this section come from Indigenous people themselves, specifically nineteenth- and twentieth-century elders who wished to record their traditions for posterity.

MODERN AND MISCELLANEOUS STORIES

Other vestiges of European fairy lore exist in New York, including the tradition of placing Christmas elf ornaments (*Jul nissen* in Danish) on mantelpieces or trees at Christmas. The Christmas elf came to these shores with the Danish who immigrated to New York State in the early twentieth century. Before being turned into the cotton or china figure we see today, the Christmas elf was a real folkloric being that lived in a family's barn and played pranks on those who didn't appease him with gifts of oats and porridge. In 1950s Troy, New York, folklorist Mildred Larson wrote that elderly Danish Americans continued to remember the elf by displaying a china or cotton figure at Christmas.

Jenny Nyström's 1896 depiction of Scandinavian Christmas elves, a supernatural being brought to these shores by Danish and other immigrants. *Public domain.*

ENERET J.F.

Besides these vestigial traditions, fairies and other Little People have sometimes crept into the great American genre of the "tall tale," a type of humorous, reality-defying story in which heroes of the American frontier perform outlandish deeds while logging, trapping and hunting. The tall tale appears in chapter 4 of this book, where I introduce famous "man of the woods" Bill Greenfield, who, according to one source, met the Little People deep in the Adirondack Mountains. I also explore hints of Welsh fairy lore brought to the towns of Steuben, Remsen and Trenton in the Adirondack foothills.

Often less traditional or even purposefully fictional, these stories add a unique flavor to New York State's fairy folklore, quite different from the more ancient stories.

I close chapter 4 with a summary of the findings of the Fairy Censuses of 2014–17 and 2017–23. I'll say more about each of these sources in the relevant sections.

Chapter 1

IRISH FAIRIES

More than any other non-Indigenous ethnic group, Irish immigrants have cast a lasting spell of fairy folklore over the hills and forests of the Empire State. Although some Irish immigrants in the nineteenth century claimed that the fairies would always remain on Irish soil and would never follow them across the ocean, many others continued to believe, and some even claimed to have encountered the fairies in the New World.

The geographical diversity of Irish fairy stories in the state—from New York City to the Upper Hudson Valley to the shores of Lake Ontario—is testament to how far Irish immigrants have carried their fairy beliefs. Most of these stories were first attested in the wake of the Great Famine of 1845–52, when immigration from Ireland increased dramatically. Before that, the Irish had begun to migrate to America but not in such numbers that they made a noticeable impression on recorded folklore. In the post-famine era, we find widespread evidence of belief in banshees in Manhattan and Queens. Beliefs about other types of fairies, including changelings, will-o'-the-wisps and Little People (such as the leprechaun and *far darrig*), are also found throughout the state at this time.

Two types of Irish fairy stories are included in this book: stories of immigrants encountering fairies in New York State and stories of those who encountered fairies in Ireland before coming here. While the former are clearly the most important stories for the purpose of this book, I believe that the latter play an important role because they represent an American (albeit imported) tradition of fairy belief. Furthermore, both types of stories happened to New Yorkers, whether before or after their voyage to America.

BANSHEES IN NEW YORK CITY

Modern, frenetic New York City is possibly the last place you'd expect to meet an Irish fairy. In fact, for many years, folklorists generally agreed that New York's Irish Americans must have left the "fairy faith" behind them when they alighted on these shores. Away from the hills and valleys of Ireland, they tended to forget about the Little People.

In the late nineteenth century, New York City's industrial landscape was a far cry from the Emerald Isle, not only geographically but culturally and environmentally as well. The Hell's Kitchen neighborhood is a case in point. Squeezed into overcrowded tenements and living from paycheck to paycheck, the Irish of Midtown Manhattan were forced to work in some of the city's dirtiest, smelliest, most unsavory locations: fat-rendering factories, slaughterhouses, coal yards and breweries. Surrounded by so much ugliness, how could they continue to believe in fairies?

Nevertheless, a quick look at the history of Irish immigration in the city suggests that even amid the noise and bustle of a great metropolis, the fairies of Irish folklore found a home.

H.R. Heaton's depiction of the "friendly banshee" in D.R. McAnally's *Irish Wonders* (1888). *Public domain.*

Although some immigrants located the fairies exclusively in the Old Country, others placed them in the heart of the city, and even those who no longer believed in fairies continued to tell stories about them. As native New Yorker Emmett Corry of the New York Irish History Roundtable explained in 1997, one needn't have ever visited Ireland or seen a fairy to learn about the Little People: "When the old ones told their magic tales of the land," he reminisced, "about pookas and little people, the fairy rings that no one would touch…in my mind's eye, I could see the hills, streams and farms of Galway and Clare."

Corry was far from alone in his fairy-filled imaginings. Elsa Herzfeld, a sociologist who studied Hell's Kitchen's

Irish American families at the turn of the twentieth century, discovered that many immigrants continued to cherish ancient folklore decades after their arrival on these shores. One example of this lore (which, ironically, contradicts modern practices associated with St. Patrick's Day) was the immigrants' fear of wearing green, which put the wearer at risk of death. What made the color so dangerous, you ask? Its power derived, in part, from its association with the fairies, who not only wore green but were also often conflated with the dead.

One fairy whom the Hell's Kitchen Irish believed in widely was the banshee. Often described as a bitterly lamenting woman wrapped in a cloak with strands of white hair falling around her, the banshee attached herself to an old Irish family and wailed (she *keened*) when a family member was about to die. The word *banshee*, in fact, means "fairy woman," and the Irish of Hell's Kitchen depicted her in a very traditional light.

"One family," reported Herzfeld, "represented her as a woman in a trailing white dress who hovers about the precincts and wails loudly when death is approaching."

This description may sound frightening, but the banshee wasn't always a source of fear. Despite associating her with death, the same family described the banshee as a "good woman," for she never *inflicted* death, only announced it. This is consistent with Irish folklorist D.R. McAnally's 1888 portrayal of the "friendly banshee" who wore "long, white drapery" that fell "below her feet" as she floated "in the air."

Although some Hell's Kitchen residents were inclined to believe that the banshee would never come to America (she was "afraid to cross the ocean," they said), storytelling about her persisted, and this wasn't limited to Midtown Manhattan.

One example of such storytelling can be found in Blissville, a neighborhood of Long Island City, in the 1880s. Early in that decade, strange claims had begun to spread that a banshee was on the loose amid the tombstones and vaults of Calvary Cemetery, a sprawling city of the dead across the water from Manhattan. Though inspired by real-life events, the story, as we'll see, clearly drew on Irish folklore.

In the 1880s, Blissville was a rustic community, for the Queensboro Bridge that would one day connect Queens to Manhattan hadn't yet been constructed. However, a number of Irish families had moved into the area, taking jobs in the factories along Newtown Creek. These factories included a fat-rendering site, a chemical works, an oil refinery and cow stables, all of which emitted ghastly smells that settled over Blissville like a putrid cloud. Similar to Hell's Kitchen in Manhattan, Blissville was an object of disdain to members of New York's Yankee establishment, who associated it with brawls and drinking.

Blissville's banshee first appeared on the evening of March 6, 1884, when James Flaherty, a forty-nine-year-old florist from Ireland, heard a woman's cry resounding through the neighborhood while walking home through Blissville. Believing that a woman was in distress and that the cry must have issued from a derelict building, Flaherty searched the building from top to bottom but found nothing except empty rooms. He then heard the cry issuing again from a "vacant lot" behind the house. Looking out of the building's attic window, Flaherty could see that nobody was there. Feeling rather spooked, he decided to continue his way home.

At home, Flaherty told his son John what he'd heard, and John set out with a gun and a group of ten friends to investigate. They also heard the strange "soprano" cry issuing from Calvary Cemetery. Peering through the gates, one young man thought he saw a woman, but this turned out to be a tombstone (probably one of the mortuary statues found on pillars throughout the cemetery). Eventually, the group disbanded and went home.

The next night, a larger group of men gathered at the neighborhood's Bradley Hotel with plans to spread out over Blissville and investigate the noise. As soon as the investigation had begun, the men heard a cry issuing from the abandoned house and then from the nearby cemetery. After investigating both locations and finding nothing, the men were too scared to continue. At this point, almost all of them believed that the culprit was a ghost, although nobody had yet uttered the word *banshee*. "No living thing could talk like that," one man was heard to say. "It must be the voice of one that's dead."

Later that night, a man named John Powers was walking home through Blissville when he met "a little woman in the road just back of the Debevoise homestead." Powers described the woman as dressed in black, moving along "strangely" and vanishing as soon as he took his eyes off her. The sight of the woman was so "weird and unearthly," said Powers, that "his knees quaked and his heart came up into his throat." Later that night, Thomas Culvert Jr. also encountered the woman, describing her as looking about twenty-five or thirty years old, "not more than three feet tall" and with "red hair" that fell in "long curls…down her back." Her face wore an expression of "deep melancholy," and her eyes were a "stony blue" that "chilled his blood."

Monuments and tombstones in Calvary Cemetery, Queens, where legend says the Blissville Banshee roamed at night. *Author's photo.*

Powers's and Culvert's woman in black is rather unlike a traditional banshee. However, the descriptions of their encounters, especially Culvert's claim that the woman had a rare combination of red hair and blue eyes, inevitably suggested to the Blissville community that just such a being had visited their neighborhood. The haunting soprano cries, heard by so many, reinforced this belief, and when an unnamed Irishman reminded his fellow citizens of the following piece of lore, everyone's mind was set: "In the Old Country," he said, "when the banshee came around, the handsomest girl in the neighborhood was sure to die. I don't mean to say that—God forbid it—but it doesn't look right to me."

From this point on, the being haunting Blissville became known as the "Blissville Banshee," a moniker the *New York Times* picked up and deployed, to humorous effect, in a handful of sensational stories.

Once the banshee was named as such, she quickly entered the Blissville psyche, her story shrouded in myth and legend. Books and local websites began to repeat the tale, and the story took on a life of its own, the banshee's presence reported sometimes in the streets of Blissville, sometimes in Calvary Cemetery and sometimes on Newtown Creek. As Mitch Waxman, historian at the Newtown Creek Alliance, wrote in 2013, the story of the banshee metastasized "over the years, and as the legend evolved, the Blissville Banshee ended up taking to the waters....She was described as floating along on a raft of mist, uttering her horrible cries, and utterly terrifying the laborers and residents of Blissville."

Newtown Creek in Queens with the Manhattan skyline in the distance. The creek is one location where the Blissville Banshee has been sighted. *Author's photo.*

According to one tongue-in-cheek account from historian Bob Singleton, the banshee's presence could even be blamed for the breakdown of Blissville's residential ethos, for it was only after she came to Blissville that the neighborhood declined, becoming ring-fenced for manufacturing, which means that no homes can be built there now.

As an addendum to the story, I should point out that some members of the Blissville community attempted to pin the blame for the cries on members of the African American community. Those accused of making the sounds (supposedly engaging in a prank) always denied the accusations, and one man even took his accuser to court. Others blamed the noises on an owl or young boys, but no one could explain the mysterious presence of the black-garbed, three-foot woman.

FAIRIES ON A BROOKLYN ROOF

Few people would describe belief in fairies as a symptom of mental illness. However, the belief does occasionally become entwined with illness in such a way that folkloric ideas become indistinguishable from psychopathology. This is true of the Irishwoman Mary Nell, a resident of Manhattan in the 1860s who believed her son was a fairy changeling (we'll learn more about her case later). It's also true of John Stanton, a man who, in 1880, shot an Anglican nun in Manhattan's Lower East Side because he believed she consorted with malicious fairies. According to one report from the *New York Herald*, which may or may not be reliable, Stanton said that "witches and fairies control Long Island, and they have often misplaced the switches along the railroad."

It's in the context of these stories that I wish to point out the curious tale of a Brooklyn man who believed he saw fairies dancing outside his bedroom window. The man's visions took place a short time before Blissville's banshee haunting, and despite the fact that fairy belief was common among New York Irishmen at this time (that is, it wasn't limited to the mentally ill), one writer, reflecting on the case in the *Journal of Nervous and Mental Diseases*, described the man as a "hallucinated lunatic." Perhaps understandably, fairy visions in 1880s New York were far more likely to be interpreted through the lens of psychiatry than folklore.

The story of our Brooklyn visionary didn't appear first in the pages of a medical journal. A Brooklyn police superintendent, Edwin Campbell (a first-generation Scottish American), told the story to a reporter at the *New York Sun*. A man in his district had come to him one day to complain about a "crowd of fairies" congregating on a roof outside his window. They were "little people of both sexes," he said, "about two or three feet tall, dressed in fantastic costumes and with funny faces." They made such a noise at night—chattering, dancing and pulling faces at him—that the man rarely slept and often felt exhausted. He hoped the superintendent would get rid of them for him.

In Campbell's account of the interview, far from labeling the man a "hallucinated lunatic," he called the fairy visions a "vagary"—in other words, out of keeping with the man's overall personality. In every sense except this one, said Campbell, the man appeared like other men, "active," "successful" and of a "sound" mind. He'd even "put off speaking about the fairies" for as long as possible and only made the complaint when he felt "annoyed almost to death." It wasn't until a medical journal published the man's story that his fairy visions became evidence of outright "lunacy."

Rather than dismissing the man, Campbell thought it best to play along with the "delusion." The strategy worked for a while: He promised the man he'd put a stop to the fairies' activities and assured him he'd no longer see them on his roof. "You go to bed to-night and go to sleep," he said, "and you'll hear no more of the fairies."

The man went away, and three months passed during which the superintendent believed the problem was fixed. Unfortunately, the man returned saying that "the same old fairies" were back and noisier than ever. "After you drove them off," he said, referring to Campbell's trickery, "I didn't hear or see anything more of them until last night when they came back again." This second visit ended in much the same way as the first, with Campbell promising the man he'd attend to the matter and the man leaving satisfied.

If the man's visions really were a "hallucination" and sign of "lunacy," as the writer in the *Journal of Nervous and Mental Diseases* suggested, one might conclude that the trappings of fairy folklore had become attached to the man's mental illness. His description of the fairies—from their size to their behavior to the clothes they wore—certainly matches fairies found in Irish and British folklore. Nevertheless, it's odd that the man brought the matter to the police. Folklore describes many charms against fairies, and according to academic Meredith Linn, New York City's Irish immigrants possessed an understanding of "magical iron cures" (that is, the use of iron objects to ward off supernatural threats). If the man's description of the fairies reflected a familiarity with fairy folklore, one might expect him to make use of such a remedy. But as a modern man in a modern city, his faith in the police evidently outweighed any faith he had in magical interventions.

THE FAIRY SPRING OF PATERSON

Leaving New York City and traveling twenty miles west, we find that fairy folklore has taken root in the suburbs as much as it has in the metropolis. That's because a miraculous fairy spring (or so the legend goes) once rose at the corner of Mill and Oliver Streets in Paterson, New Jersey, where it provided fresh water to the city's nineteenth-century Irish immigrants. Now a major suburb of New York City, back then Paterson was a thriving mill town, its industrial power deriving from a much larger source of water: the giant waterfall on the Passaic River, which raged—and still rages—at the heart of the city.

The Irish who came to draw water from the spring arrived in the early nineteenth century in Paterson, where they hoped to build lives for themselves in the land of opportunity. Their numbers increased after the Great Irish Famine of 1845–52, when millions of people fled Ireland in an attempt to escape hunger and mass evictions. By 1888, they accounted for most of the city's industrial laborers, many working in silk mills along the river. They soon formed a neighborhood, dubbed Little Dublin, at the foot of Garett Mountain, where they lived in tenement housing. It was this neighborhood that gave the spring its name: the Dublin Spring. These poor but industrious workers could frequently be seen lining up at the spring to collect water for cooking and bathing.

When I say the spring was a fairy spring, I'm referring to an ancient legend, the origin of which is lost in the mists of Paterson's early history. According to an old Irish American man quoted in the *Paterson Evening News* on October 27, 1900, the spring's "fairy nature" can be attributed to its legendary origin, which was widely known throughout Little Dublin in the nineteenth century.

The legend suggests that a fairy, taking pity on the Irish who lived in such humble abodes so very far away from home, took up water from the Lakes of Killarney (a beautiful series of crystalline lakes on Ireland's southwestern tip) and placed them in her apron. She then flew three thousand miles across

The *Water Boy* sculpture by Gaetano Federici, commemorating the Dublin Spring that rose in Paterson, New Jersey. Dedicated in 1931. *Author's photo.*

the Atlantic Ocean to plant the waters beneath Little Dublin. Once the waters were planted there, said the old man, they became "an everlasting source of pure and sweet water for the lads and lassies from the emerald isle."

Over the years, "dozens" of other legends also developed in association with the spring, lending it a sacred aura. One example of this lore was the belief that lovers who drank the spring's water from the same cup on Halloween night (known as "Holly Eve") would never be parted. Another was that if a man drank from the spring's innermost part or "recess," he'd never leave Paterson except under the "fairy influence"; if he did, the same fairy or "nymph" would surely bring him back again. Besides these fanciful tales, the spring—accessed via a set of stone steps—always ran clean, and sometimes as many as fifty people could be seen waiting in line to collect water.

Many of these legends have deep roots in Irish folklore, especially the story of the water-bearing fairy and the spring's association with romance. Echoes of the lore contained in these tales can be found in an ancient legend about the origins of the Lakes of Killarney, a story Paterson's Irish immigrants may well have known by heart. Told in Ireland since time immemorial, the legend (one version of it anyway) is preserved in the writings of English poet Thomas Haynes Bayly.

Bayly explained that long ago, the valley of Killarney was full of bogs and fens. The peasants who lived there had to make do with just one spring to satisfy all their needs. Known as a "fairy spring" for its health-giving properties and the fact that it never ran dry, it was similar in many ways to other Irish springs: after people drew the water, they always placed a stone over the spring's head to protect it from contamination. Those who forgot to replace the stone risked bringing down a terrible misfortune on themselves and their unsuspecting neighbors.

In Bayly's legend, the fairy who lived in the spring placed a giant stone over its head and arranged, by means of fairy enchantment, that only the valley's

Photograph of the Lakes of Killarney, entitled "In the Upper Lake, Killarney, County Kerry, Ireland." Published between 1890 and 1900. *Public domain.*

maidens would be able to lift it. One day, a beautiful maiden had gone to the spring to draw water when she met a young man with whom she fell deeply in love. When the man asked her to follow him home, the maiden agreed, forgetting all about the stone and leaving the spring uncovered. The maid's absentmindedness enraged the spring's fairy so much that she caused the spring to burst forth with violence. It eventually flooded the valley, creating the Lakes of Killarney.

How does this older legend relate to that of the Dublin Spring?

The man who shared the Paterson legends also mentioned the origin of the Killarney lakes, but he changed the story slightly. Instead of flooding the valley in anger, the fairy in the man's amended version only created the lakes because she pitied the peasants who lived there, forced to survive on just one spring. Despite this, the peasants grumbled at the fairy, complaining that the lakes had covered their "bogs and fens." "They had no eye" for the water's beauty, the fairy concluded. In response, she placed the Killarney waters in her apron and carried them over to Paterson. The people of the Irish diaspora would be grateful for the water, she said, for they knew how to appreciate beauty.

BY 1900, WHEN THE *Paterson Evening News* ran its story on Paterson's Irish legends, the condition of the Dublin Spring's waters had irrevocably changed. Industrialists and modernizers, the writer claimed, had transformed Paterson—covering up its brooks, polluting its springs and installing "ugly wooden pumps" to collect its waters. To make matters worse, the legendary fairies and nymphs of the spring had fled. This was the writer's poetic way of explaining that Paterson had lost its charm and that the creation of an artificial environment had severed the town's citizens from the beauty of nature. The fairies, he said, had found a refuge in the waters of Betty's Falls, northwest of Paterson in the Ramapo Mountains. They'd "spread their wings" and flown away, seeking out new "resting places in the glens and… cascades, in the mountains to the north."

Unfortunately, the situation of the spring today is even more dire than it was in 1900, for construction has completely covered it over. Those who wish to pay their respects to the fairy of the spring may still do so, however, at the Ward Street sculpture of the *Water Boy*, a figure depicted in bronze collecting water from the spring. Installed in Paterson in 1931, the statue is a truly joyous one—a fitting memorial to the Irish community and a constant reminder of the connection existing between the waters of Paterson and the Lakes of Killarney.

Whether Paterson's nineteenth-century Irish really believed in fairies (like their kin in Manhattan and Queens) or merely enjoyed telling a good story, the legend of the Dublin Spring demonstrates that they kept the old-world folklore alive even in the midst of the Industrial Revolution. Besides, the story of the spring wasn't Paterson's only fairy legend. Another piece of folk wisdom found in the town was the rumor that a fairy appeared sometimes in Paterson, walking through the streets of Little Dublin, a "tottering old woman begging with a cane." The historian Herbert Gutman argued that such "mythic beliefs" served to "cement" the collective identity of Paterson's Irish immigrants and to ensure that the community expressed "concern for the elderly and disabled." In the town's rapidly industrializing culture, concern for the weak and vulnerable was a must.

CHANGELINGS

The fairies we've met so far in this book have been largely unthreatening—frightening, certainly, but not inflicting major harm. Other fairies are more pernicious, and few are as horrifying as the fairy who steals children, leaving changelings in their place. Stories about changelings are found in locations throughout New York, including the forests north of Albany, the Finger Lakes in western New York and New York City itself. While folklorists have sometimes claimed that only one case of a fairy changeling has been identified in New York, this isn't exactly true. Only one case has ever been *authenticated* (that of Mary Nell, which we'll examine soon), but New York folklore contains a handful of references to the phenomenon, some more reliable than others. New York residents who've referred to fairy changelings may have occasionally dealt in hearsay, but the storytellers themselves are often easy to identify, lending a concrete credibility to their accounts. Their experiences (or those of their loved ones and neighbors) attest to the survival of fairy changeling folklore in New York well into the late Victorian age.

The first story I relate here took place in Lisha's Kill, an old Dutch community situated amid ancient forests north of Albany and so named for the creek that passes through the village.

One day in the mid-1870s, Lisha's Kill resident John Marman, a carpenter and first-generation Irish American, sat down in his rocking chair beside a crib where his son was sleeping. Before dozing off, John noticed movement in the crib: something was tugging at the baby's "bed clothes." Jumping up, John yelled hoarsely, and immediately the tugging ceased. He watched, alert for movement in the shadows, when suddenly he saw "a tiny bit of a wee girl" scampering "out of the room through the keyhole." Apparently, John Marman had just seen a fairy.

These are the events John related in the 1890s to his granddaughter May Quinn (née Brooks) of Albany, New York, when she was just a little girl. In the 1940s, May related to a folklorist what her grandfather had told her, thereby vouching for the grandfather's long-held belief in fairies.

John Marman had apparently been convinced that the "wee" fairy was about to steal his son George and replace him with a "fairy changeling"—one of the fairies' sickly children, whom John and his wife, Julia, would be forced to raise as their own. Cases of fairy changeling belief are rare in North America, though certainly not unheard of. Occurring more often in Ireland, they offered parents a framework for understanding why an otherwise healthy child would become suddenly ill or disabled: a fairy must have stolen the child and substituted a fairy baby.

One way to rectify the situation was to place the child on a red-hot shovel or apply an iron object to its skin. This caused the fairy (who hated the fire

T.H. Thomas's depiction of fairies stealing a woman's baby, as found in Wirt Sikes's *British Goblins* (1880). *Public domain.*

and the iron object) to fly away, leaving the original child in its place. As you can imagine, this so-called treatment led to tragic, untimely deaths.

Although discrepancies exist between the tale as May told it and the historical events of her grandfather's life, the story nevertheless offers a fascinating glimpse into the survival of fairy folklore in late nineteenth-century New York. It also suggests that some Irish Americans located fairies in North America itself.

The case of John Marman is probably the most innocuous example of fairy changeling belief in New York State. A much darker example comes to us from Port Leyden, deep in the forests of northern New York. According to a Maine-born woman called Martina O'Brien (née Harriman), who lived near Port Leyden in the 1910s and 1920s, an Irishwoman who lived in the town came to believe that fairies had stolen her child while she was out picking blackberries. The folklorist who reported the story claimed that the woman "felt no obligation to raise the child of the fairies, especially since they had taken away her own." As a result, the child was "neglected" and finally "died."

Author Mason Winfield mentioned a similar case of a fairy changeling in the town of Victor, north of the Finger Lakes. He described an Irish couple who hired many laborers to tend to their large estate in the town, situated "where today's Interstate 90 meets and obliterates the landscape of the old Route 96." Because the marshes around the estate glowed an "eerie green" at night, spooking the Irish farmhands, the estate became known as the "Fairy Farm." Confirming the farmhands' suspicion that fairies were inhabiting the area, the owners of the farm gave birth to a girl with Down's syndrome, whom they "tragically" suspected of being a fairy changeling. Although Winfield doesn't explain what happened to the girl, based on other cases of changeling belief, it likely wasn't good.

I turn now to the most famous, tragic and violent case of a New York fairy changeling—the story of Mary Nell, a thirty-eight-year-old Irishwoman who lived on Manhattan's Upper West Side in the 1860s. At that time, the Upper West Side was a ramshackle neighborhood of cheaply constructed houses sought out by low-income Irish and other immigrant families displaced from Central Manhattan by the creation of Central Park. Later, apartment buildings came to exist side by side with the neighborhood's shacks and cabins, and it was in one such building that Mary Nell lived with her three-year-old son, John, and husband, Matthias. Based on an article about Mary that appeared in the *New York Times* on March 18, 1863, it appears she had a strange relationship with a man who'd formerly lived in her building, for he managed to convince her that fairies were haunting the residence.

As the *New York Times* reported, "Before coming to this country from Ireland, [the] witness was taught the common superstition of her country, that whenever '*fairies*' frequented a house it was presumptive evidence that some child in the family had been changed for another while in its cradle." Fairy-folklore expert Simon Young, in his analysis of the Mary Nell case, explained that the newspaper's characterization of Irish changeling belief is inconsistent with nineteenth-century folklore (the presence of fairies, for example, is not, in itself, a guarantee that a child will be taken). Nevertheless, Mary's belief in fairy changelings—combined with the stress of caring for her son in the absence of her husband (who'd recently joined a Civil War regiment bound for Washington, D.C.)—apparently convinced her that young John was just such a being.

The tragic denouement of the story occurred not long after Mary's husband, Matthias, deserted from his post in the army and left Riker's Island, where his regiment was stationed, to return to Manhattan. He later claimed he was worried about his wife acting "strangely," and it may well have been his fears for her safety that impelled him to return to his home. Despite this, Matthias wasn't present on the fateful day when his wife took young John and placed him on a heated spade, hoping to drive the fairy out. This resulted in poor John dying one week later from severe burns and Mary being confined to the New York Lunatic Asylum on Roosevelt Island.

Of all the cases of fairy changelings uncovered in New York, Mary Nell's is clearly the most horrific. Like the case of the woman in Port Leyden who allowed her baby to starve, it's also incredibly tragic. Presumably found innocent by reason of insanity, Mary Nell later lived as a widow in Manhattan. Her name has since gone down in history as representative of fairy folklore's darkest aspect.

HUGH DUFFY MEETS THE FAIRIES

Not all fairies in Irish American folklore are diminutive beings. Although the Blissville Banshee was thought to be a three-foot woman and John Marman's fairy was so small she could fit through a keyhole, other fairies, such as the banshees of Hell's Kitchen, were more likely to be human sized, in keeping with descriptions from Irish folklore. That being said, when folklorist Louis C. Jones collected the stories of New York's Irish Americans in 1945, he found widespread belief in Little People. New Yorkers tended to locate these Little People in the Old Country rather than the New. In other words, they mainly failed to cross the ocean.

One exception to this rule can be seen in an entry dated April 24, 1887, in the diary of William Connelly, an Irishman who lived in the town of Greece, a suburb of Rochester near Lake Ontario. The entry is important because it's one of the few vivid descriptions of an Irish American encounter with fairies in New York in the nineteenth century, and so I quote it here in full:

> *April 24, 1887—Young Hughey Duffy saw the "Fairies" last night, so he says. They were dancing at the crossroads just as they do in Ireland. Hughey had been in Charlotte during the afternoon, where he purchased an iron kettle. He attended the Preston wake and was walking out Latta Road in the small hours of the morning. He encountered the "Fairies" at the corner of the road that goes down to Pat Fleming's. They were a number of the "little people," and Hughey thinking they were children was about to stop and ask what they were doing out at that hour when one of them cried, "Stand aside all and let Master Duffy pass with his iron pot and pot-hooks." With that they disappeared as though the ground had opened for them. Hughey broke into a run, nor did he stop until he had reached Slater's driveway.*

To add some context to the events described, I should point out that Greece in 1887 was a rural farming community. Both men, Hugh Duffy and William Connelly, lived in farming households. At night, the town would have been particularly quiet and conducive to fairy activity. The young "Hughey Duffy" was most likely the same Hugh Duffy Jr. who lived with his father, Hugh Duffy Sr., in Greece in 1892. Both men, like Connelly, were Irish-born immigrants to the United States, the younger Hugh being about thirty-five.

Before taking a closer look at Hugh's experience, I'd like to draw attention to one detail in Connelly's reporting that may influence how we perceive the event:

Connelly explained that Hugh had been returning from the "Preston wake" on the night he met the fairies—a reference to Julia Farnan Preston, a widow who died on April 22, the day before Hugh's encounter. Nineteenth-century Irish wakes sometimes went on for days, with neighbors and relatives coming and going, indulging in merriment, games and drinking to support the people in mourning. It's possible that Hugh, returning home at such an hour, had consumed a fair amount of liquor. This might explain Connelly's use of the expression "so he says" when introducing Hugh's tale. Although being drunk or "tipsy" doesn't necessarily lessen the credibility of Hugh's story, it's suggestive of the state of mind he may have been in while walking home in the "small hours of the morning."

It's also worth mentioning that the fairies were dancing at a crossroads in the middle of the night.

John Dickson Batten's illustration of one of the Irish Little People from *Celtic Fairy Tales* (1892). *Public domain.*

Crossroads dancing was a popular activity in rural Ireland, the open spaces where two or three roads meet providing an ideal location for gatherings. Roads were far less busy than they are today, especially in the countryside, and it was common to see young men and women walking out on summer evenings to gather at a crossroads to dance. The activity was considered safe and sociable because it mainly took place before dark.

In stark contrast, the fairies in Hugh's story were dancing at a totally inhospitable hour, thereby revealing their otherworldly nature. Fairies in Hugh's day were evidently seen as somewhat similar to human beings but also somewhat unnatural, performing their activities in the dead of night. Hugh's rational response to meeting them—his flight—is testament to the eeriness of their behavior.

Despite this obvious strangeness, Hugh's fairies are quite familiar figures. They were clearly *Irish* fairies because they behaved remarkably similarly to the fairies of Irish folklore, not only dancing at crossroads but also fearing iron, which caused them to pay their respects to Hugh before vanishing. One can't help wondering if encountering such a potent emblem of Ireland in his home across the ocean was, in some sense, rather comforting for Hugh.

MORE LITTLE PEOPLE LORE

Hugh Duffy's fairy encounter didn't take place in a vacuum. In fact, a wealth of Little People beliefs existed among nineteenth-century New Yorkers. Folklorist Louis Jones found that the "fairy faith" was so strong in 1940s New York that many people claimed to have either encountered the fairies in person or known people who'd seen them. Many of these stories date to the nineteenth or early twentieth centuries, and they nearly always take place on Irish soil: Hugh Duffy and John Marman were among the few Irish immigrants who actually saw the Little People in New York.

Here I offer a brief summary of New Yorkers' experiences in Ireland as well as their beliefs about the Little People more generally. For many of these stories, we're indebted to the work of Louis Jones and his students.

The first interesting case of Little People belief comes to us from a woman called Anna Jones who lived in Saratoga Springs. She spoke of friends in Cork who claimed to have received visits from the *far darrig* ("red man" in English), a fairy she described as having a "little red hat and gray hair," a "red coat and gray britches" and "brogues with big silver buckles on them."

This fairy was thought to knock on farmers' doors and ask if he could come in to enjoy some rest. Whoever opened the door would find a "tiny, dried up man" who'd immediately rush "into the house" and sit beside the fire smoking a pipe. The hospitable souls who welcomed the far darrig were sure to receive good luck.

Other New York residents, lacking firsthand experience of the fairies, nevertheless shared vivid descriptions of them. A common thread in these descriptions is the fairies' penchant for wearing the colors red and green. According to one believer, anyone who looked out of the window on the eve of St. Patrick's Day in Ireland was sure to see the fairies "marching north in long lines, each one dressed in red coat and green pants." Another informant described the fairies as "always dressed in red" with "red caps" or "red coats and white pants."

The leprechaun, of course, was a particular object of belief for some New Yorkers, their descriptions of him adhering quite closely to traditional Irish belief. He was a little shoemaker, they said, who'd been working "since the dawn of time" and hiding his earnings in secret treasure-troves. If you caught the leprechaun and held him tight, he was bound to share his treasure with you; otherwise, you could catch him with a woolen thread or a "plough chain." If you kept your eyes on him at all times, he'd dig up his treasure and give it to you, but he was also a master of distraction, so he usually made sure that anyone who beheld him would eventually look away, giving him time to escape.

Besides the far darrig and the leprechaun, New Yorkers described other fairies too who, despite remaining unseen, caused them to wander for hours at night not recognizing familiar sights. Strangely enough, this phenomenon may have been more likely to occur to an immigrant on the eve of their departure for America.

One man called Kyran McGarrity, a steamfitter from Albany who hailed from Ireland's County Laois, said that the night before he sailed for New York in 1903, he was following his usual route home across the fields when the fairies began to lead him in "circles and zigzags," making him "more and more confused." This continued for some time until he was finally able to grope "his way through the opening in the hedge."

A similar experience occurred to a great-aunt of May Quinn on the evening before she sailed for New York. (May was the granddaughter of John Marman, whom we met in the section on changelings.) The aunt had been visiting friends to say her goodbyes and was returning home when the fairies caused her to keep "walking and walking" but getting "nowhere." Despite being able to see her home, she "could make no progress" and was only able to escape the spell when the dawn came and she realized she was "miles from her home." In his reporting of the story, Louis Jones remarked that "no doubt," the fairies "hated to see another fine Irish girl leaving the land that bore her."

FAIRY FIRES

A less common but nevertheless fascinating feature of New York fairy folklore is the phenomenon of fairies manifesting as small bright lights or "fairy fires" that move mysteriously through the landscape. The tendency to see fairies as disembodied flames is especially common among the findings of the Fairy Census (reported at the end of this book). It's also found, to a lesser extent, among Irish immigrants of the nineteenth century.

Manifestations of fairy fires have occurred as far west as Rochester. However, the example I wish to share with you now occurred farther east in the Mohawk Valley—Herkimer County to be precise.

If you head north from the town of Herkimer with the West Canada Creek on your right, you'll eventually come to the old Kast Bridge, beyond which (on the right) is a haunted wetland where a notoriously dangerous will-o'-the-wisp was thought to chase people who strayed too close to its swampy home.

Will-o'-the-wisps are eerie blue, red or bright white lights that hover over swamps and marshes. Scientists have generally concluded that decaying bacteria create the lights when they emit a gas that burns on contact with the air. Others claim the lights are a supernatural phenomenon called a fairy fire. One Irish explanation is that the light shines from the lantern of a man named Will Cooper who was cursed to wander in search of a home but finding none, his lantern burning with a coal from hell.

Although will-o'-the-wisps were not usually considered to be that dangerous in Ireland, they did sometimes lure people into swamps and marshes, causing them to become lost or stuck. It's only in North America, however, that they've been known to chase people. According to Louis Jones, the Irish Americans of Herkimer County feared Kast's Swamp's "red ball with a fiery tail" because they knew that if it caught up with them, they'd suffer a sudden death.

Legend suggests this happened once to an unfortunate man who lived near the bridge over West Canada Creek. One day, he went to get milk from Kast's Farm, taking a shortcut through the swamp. Bad idea! The will-o'-the-wisp rose up from the murky depths and took off after him. Terrified, he ran toward his home, and just when he'd reached his door, "the evil fairy caught up with him." As soon as the man opened the door, he fell down dead on the doorstep.

Another type of fairy fire found elsewhere in New York—mentioned in the nineteenth-century diary of William Connelly—is the "death light."

THE IGNIS-FATUUS, OR WILL-O'-THE-WISP.

Wood engraving by C.H. Whymper showing an *ignis fatuus* or will-o'-the-wisp. *Public domain.*

Described in a history of Rochester's Our Mother of Sorrows Church as a "strange yellow [sphere]" or "little dancing [globe] of light," it appeared often at night around the town of Greece.

What could have earned this fire such a morbid name? Presumably, Connelly called it a death light because old legends had suggested to him that the light appeared when someone was about to die. In fact, Father Robert McNamara, historian of Our Mother of Sorrows Church, said the light "did appear, more than once, just before a death in the neighborhood." The phenomenon is similar to the "death candle" of Welsh folklore, a glowing orb thought to appear before the death of a local resident.

A handful of descriptions of the death light can be found in Connelly's diary. One of his most memorable sightings occurred one night as the light was crossing the highway near his home. The diarist, curious, tried to approach it, but it "moved too quickly," forcing him to retreat. On another occasion, he wanted to draw near the light, but a kitten crossed back and forth in front of him, preventing him from moving toward it. The implication seems to be that the kitten, displaying an animal's clairvoyance, had saved Connelly's life.

NOT ALL STORIES ABOUT fairy fires concern disembodied flames like the will-o'-the-wisp or death light; sometimes the fairies need to *build* fires as the focal point for their dancing. This type of fairy fire can be seen in the report of an Irishwoman called Annie Hannan (née Carey) from Glens Falls, Warren County, who described encountering a fairy fire before coming to America in 1903. This tale is an example of a fairy encounter in Ireland becoming a story in Upstate New York.

It was the end of the nineteenth century, and Annie was driving into Brandon, County Cork, to attend the fair with her mother, Mary, and brother Connie (short for Cornelius) when they saw ahead of them "a huge bonfire reaching up to the sky." It was three o'clock in the morning, a perfect time for fairies, and Connie was afraid to go on, but his mother told him to continue. When they arrived at the site where they'd seen the bonfire, to their surprise, they couldn't see one anywhere, but all along the road, they spied men dressed in black pants and white shirts (as if they'd been "laid out" for a funeral, said Annie). They were leaning on their elbows, as if exhausted. The family watched the men as they passed in the wagon, but nobody said a word. It wasn't until the family drew level with the final man that the stranger said, "Fine night." Cornelius responded, "Yes, it is."

Much later, it dawned on Annie's mother that the men "must have been the good people, resting after dancing about their bonfire."

THE HOBGOBLIN OF FORT NIAGARA

Gray and weather-beaten Fort Niagara has stood on the southwest shore of Lake Ontario since 1726—a grim reminder of the wars that raged among France, Great Britain and the United States. Built by the French to defend its colonies from the British and captured by American forces in the late eighteenth century, the fort has since accrued the dubious distinction of being among New York's most fairy-haunted locations.

The folklore that has circulated about the fort over the last few decades suggests that a young Irish American piper, stationed at the fort in 1804,

COPYRIGHT 1900 BY DETROIT PHOTOGRAPHIC CO.
012142. OLD FORT NIAGARA.
012142 OLD FORT NIAGARA.

Photograph taken inside Fort Niagara in about 1900. *Library of Congress.*

encountered a terrifying hobgoblin in an isolation cell there. The cell—which still exists—is a dank prison buried inside the fort's guardhouse. It's called, aptly, the "black hole," because, in the absence of a candle or lantern, whoever occupied the prison at night was plunged into absolute darkness.

According to New York official Samuel DeVeaux, our unfortunate piper—one John Carroll—was in the habit of drinking too freely from "Bacchus's cup," meaning he liked his wine and whiskey. One day he appeared drunk on parade and swore at his superiors. As a result, Carroll spent a night in the hole and was found in the early hours making "the most dismal sounds" and in a "piteous condition." Over the years, popular folklore has spun the tale of his incarceration into the story of an encounter with the "hobgoblin of Fort Niagara," a mysterious being that's never quite described and only vaguely defined. (In author Mason Winfield's words, it's a "goblin but more hobby.")

So, did John Carroll really meet a hobgoblin in the prison of Fort Niagara? In reality, the events are a bit more complicated than they appear. Carroll never actually said he'd met a *real* hobgoblin but that he'd been "visited by *all the hobgoblins*, and *all the devils in existence*" (my emphasis). These hobgoblins and devils "came to him immediately" upon entering the cell and "haunted him all the while he had been confined."

Based on Carroll's own words, the hobgoblins and devils were an amorphous crowd. Rather than meeting one supernatural creature (as folklore has suggested ever since), the piper appeared to be referring to a state of psychological haunting, the hobgoblins and devils being embodiments of his fear. This was a man thrown into darkness and isolation while experiencing the effects of delirium tremens (alcohol withdrawal). We know Carroll drank too much: "Of all things," wrote DeVeaux, he was "devoted to music and whisky." We also know that Niagara's drinking culture was notorious, its taverns and bordellos within easy reach of the fort. Taken together, these facts suggest that Carroll's delirium was responsible for his nighttime experience rather than a supernatural being.

Before skeptics conclude that this should put an end to the matter, I ought to note that within ten years, another soldier stationed at the fort claimed to have seen the hobgoblin. On duty near the fort's graveyard in 1812, this soldier said he encountered the monster during a lightning storm. The frightening figure appeared in a flash of lightning, causing the man to fire his rifle and flee. Unfortunately, he knocked himself out against a barricade as he went.

Whatever we might say about this second story, John Carroll clearly wasn't the only serviceman who used the word *hobgoblin* to describe a strange encounter at the fort. So could there be some truth to the supernatural explanation?

Unfortunately, the second soldier's story also raises many questions. When the soldier's superiors searched the man's quarters, they found them smelling strongly of spirits and full of empty bottles. In keeping with what we know about the fort and its men, this soldier, too, was apparently a raging alcoholic. Although the man's drunkenness doesn't necessarily rule out the existence of the hobgoblin, the evidence suggests that drinking played some role in his vision. The man's testimony becomes even shakier when we take the conditions in which he saw the being into account (it was at night during a thunderstorm).

Perhaps the most interesting thing about the story of the Fort Niagara hobgoblin is what it reveals about the vocabulary used by Irish Americans to describe fairies in the early nineteenth century. It should be noted that Carroll, presumably a proud Irish American, didn't actually encounter an Irish fairy: a hobgoblin is a being of English folklore. Composed of two words, *hob* and *goblin* (neither of which is Irish), *hobgoblin* denoted a household spirit that was troublesome or helpful, as the case may be. Carroll was clearly an English speaker and was somewhat conversant in English fairy lore. But as a man of Irish descent, he may also have been familiar with the *pooka*, another household spirit more commonly found in Irish culture. *Pooka* is related to the hobgoblin Robin Goodfellow via the name *Puck* found in Shakespeare.

One possibility is that Carroll didn't use the word *hobgoblin* at all but evoked a word such as *pooka* to describe his experience in the hole. It was Samuel DeVeaux, not Carroll himself, who recorded the story of Carroll's solitary confinement. DeVeaux may well have substituted the word *hobgoblin* for an unfamiliar Irish term. In fact, Carroll may even have had a special reason to invoke the pooka, for according to Irish lore, a pooka had the power to bestow unsurpassed mastery of

Depiction of a pooka in Wirt Sikes's *British Goblins* (1880), supposedly a copy of a Welsh peasant's drawing made in coal. *Public domain.*

the pipe. According to DeVeaux, Carroll did compose a tune in response to his experience of confinement, a "beautiful, but mournful air" that he called "Carroll's Thoughts on Eternity." Later folklore has suggested that Carroll learned the tune at the hobgoblin's insistence, a notion with strong precedent in Irish, Scottish and Welsh folklore, where fairies have been known to teach their music to mortals. Perhaps a musically gifted Irish fairy did, then, lurk behind Fort Niagara's hobgoblin. This is speculation on my part, of course.

Finally, who was John Carroll? Other than being a piper and a composer of Irish-flavored dance tunes, not much is known about him. Samuel DeVeaux speculated that he was "brother or cousin to Carroll, the famous Irish harper"—presumably a reference to Turlough O'Carolan.

It seems more likely to me that he was a relative of Maryland's Irish Catholic Carroll family, which produced one of the signers of the Declaration of Independence and America's first Catholic bishop. I make this connection because the tune Carroll composed, supposedly at the hobgoblin's request, was found among papers at Charles Carroll House, the family's seat. A recording of "Carroll's Thoughts on Eternity" can be heard on the album *Music of the Charles Carroll Family*.

Chapter 2

DUTCH GOBLINS AND GNOMES

Long before the English and Irish settled in New York, a wealthy Dutch colony called New Netherland thrived on the island of Manhattan and along the Hudson River, powered by a lucrative fur trade between the imperial powers. It all began in 1609, when Henry Hudson, an English explorer in the pay of the Dutch West India Company, headed the crew of the *Halve Maen* ("Half Moon") and traveled up the river that would one day bear his name. The ship reached as far as present-day Albany, laying the foundation for future Dutch settlements along the Hudson River, including the wealthy patroonship known as Rensselaerswick, a territory owned and governed by the wealthy Van Rensselaer family. Many of the stories gathered in this chapter take place on land once owned by the Van Rensselaers, including present-day Albany (then called Fort Orange) and the Hudson Highlands (where Dutch names such as *Dunderberg* and *Pollopel* populate our fairy stories). Other stories take place farther afield in the once exclusively Dutch Catskills, a mountainous region made famous, partly, by the story of Rip Van Winkle.

Although it's certainly true that we'll meet Dutch fairies in this section of the book—including mischievous goblins along the Hudson River, magical gnomes in the Catskill Mountains, a hobgoblin in an old Dutch church and a dwarf whose abode was Albany's Van Rensselaer Mansion—these are not fairies pulled straight from the tales of old Dutch storytellers. Almost all the stories involving Dutch fairies in this chapter are filtered through the imagination of one decidedly non-Dutch man: Washington Irving.

Arthur Rackham's depiction of the gnome-like men of the mountain from "Rip Van Winkle" (1905). *Public domain.*

Arthur Rackham 04

The Dutch history and culture of New York State fascinated Irving, and he used it as the basis for many of his most intriguing supernatural tales, including "The Storm-Ship" and "Rip Van Winkle." Although it isn't clear exactly how much authentic Dutch fairy lore Irving incorporated in his fictions, it's generally well known that he absorbed many Dutch customs, proverbs and ghost stories while visiting Tarrytown on the Hudson River as a teenager; he may well have learned there about the ancient Dutch belief in goblins and gnomes that inspired so many folktales in the Netherlands. That being said, many of the beings we'll meet in this section are probably Irving's inventions.

As folklorist Sara Puryear Roses pointed out, Irving's gnomes may not have been lifted directly from a Dutch story overheard in the Catskills, but his descriptions of them do recall "descriptions of ancient Dutch seamen and…include many of the traditional attributes of dwarves." Dwarves were a common feature of Northern European folklore, often associated with mining, precious metals and wealth. Many other dwarf-like beings, including *kabouters* (a type of gnome) and goblins, also appear in Dutch folktales, where they perform household chores or mischievous pranks depending on how well people treat them. Both of these beings make appearances in Irving's reimaginings of Dutch traditions.

I open the Dutch section of this book with the story of the Goblin King of Dunderberg Mountain, first mentioned in Irving's 1822 "The Storm-Ship." The goblin king sprang fully formed from Irving's pages to inhabit the intemperate airs around Dunderberg Mountain; in the decades that followed, he took on a life of his own, entering the realm of Hudson River folklore. Leaving Dunderberg, we travel north along the river to investigate the Hudson Highlands' so-called goblin problem, which centers largely on Bannerman Island, an uninhabited island in the river where Dutch goblins emerge at night after the tourists have departed. Heading farther up the river, we come to Kingston, where a hobgoblin haunts the steeple of the Old Dutch Church, and Albany, where the once-glorious, long-since dismantled Van Rensselaer Mansion housed two fairy spirits at the end of the nineteenth century: a protective dwarf and a sylphlike White Lady. Finally, we head to the Catskills and learn about that region's magical gnomes, inextricably linked to the story of Rip Van Winkle. In each case, I recount the story's origins and clarify its connections to ancient Dutch traditions.

THE GOBLIN KING OF DUNDERBERG

According to an *Evening News* newspaper headline that began circulating online about five years ago, a sinister face appeared once in a cloud over Hudson Valley's Dunderberg Mountain, terrifying the residents of that picturesque region of eastern New York. It was January 1956, and the mountain in question, famous for its awesome thunderstorms, stands on the western banks of the Hudson River, where, for centuries, it welcomed boats to the Hudson Highlands from the lower Hudson Valley. The headline suggested that the sighting of the face coincided with a storm in which a ship called the SS *Cornell* had capsized. "Haunting face appears over mountain," the headline said. "Dunderberg goblin real?"

In reality, no face appeared over Dunderberg Mountain and no SS *Cornell* ever sank. Whoever made the image had pasted the outline of Lord Voldemort (of *Harry Potter* fame) in the sky over Dunderberg to create the illusion of a face. The image was a clever April Fool's hoax—too good to be true in how accurately it conjured the fixtures of Hudson Valley folklore, as well as the phenomenon of *pareidolia*—the human mind's tendency to create patterns (such as faces) out of random sensory information (such as clouds).

The image was a humorous nod to one of the Hudson River's most infamous folkloric figures: the goblin king of Dunderberg Mountain, also known as the "Heer of Dunderberg." (*Heer* means lord or gentleman in Dutch.) In a single glance, the image conveyed every trapping of the goblin king's story: a threatening presence that broods over Dunderberg, high storm winds and the sinking of a ship in the Hudson. Although a hoax, the image demonstrated how deeply the goblin king legend has penetrated the Hudson Valley psyche in the two hundred years since it first appeared.

Washington Irving was the first to put the legend of the goblin king in writing in his 1822 short story "The Storm-Ship." According to that tale, eighteenth-century traders and explorers—Dutch American citizens of New York—told stories about the goblin as they sailed the Hudson River from Manhattan to Albany. Although Irving's tale is a work of fiction and the extent to which he drew on Dutch folklore is a matter of debate, he was probably right about one thing: the Dutch almost certainly feared the Hudson Highlands for the winds and storms that raged there. Whether they personified this fear in the shape of a grumpy goblin is another story.

In Irving's tale, this goblin "potentate" lived at the top of Dunderberg Mountain, where he controlled the wind and lightning, bringing down ships that passed below his mountain home. The narrator of the story, who claimed

The mouth of the Hudson Highlands with Dunderberg Mountain, home of the goblin king, on the left. *Author's photo.*

the legend was current among Dutch sea captains in the early nineteenth century, described the goblin king in the following amusing terms:

> *The captains of the river craft talk of a little bulbous-bottomed Dutch goblin, in trunk hose and sugar-loafed hat, with a speaking trumpet in his hand, which they say keeps about the Dunderberg. They declare they have heard him, in stormy weather, in the midst of the turmoil, giving orders in Low Dutch for the piping up of a fresh gust of wind, or the rattling off of another thunder-clap. That sometimes he has been seen surrounded by a crew of little imps in broad breeches and short doublets; tumbling head-over-heels in the rack and mist, and playing a thousand gambols in the air; or buzzing like a swarm of flies about Antony's Nose; and that, at such times, the hurry-scurry of the storm was always greatest.*

As this quote demonstrates, one of the goblin king's favorite pastimes was to send winds and thunderstorms raging through the Hudson Valley, a feat he achieved by shouting Low Dutch commands at an army of imps through a "speaking trumpet." We'll hear more about these imps later, but first it should be noted that when the goblin wasn't engaged in meteorological activities, he liked to intervene more personally in a ship's passage through the Highlands, as the following tale from Irving's pen reveals.

The story concerns a Dutch skipper called Daniel Ouslesticker, a man who, according to Irving's unreliable narrator, was "never known to tell a lie." Ouslesticker claimed that he saw the goblin once sitting on the bowsprit of his boat. Immediately, he asked a Dutch pastor from the town of Esopus, a man called Von Glieson, to exorcise the being. The pastor sang a hymn to St. Nicholas, and the goblin, repulsed, flew high into the air, taking with him the pastor's wife's nightcap. In the story, the nightcap was found the next day hanging from the weathercock of the Esopus Dutch Reformed Church.

A similar event, also mentioned in "The Storm-Ship," involved a "sloop" encountering trouble on the river and the goblin sending a "thunder-gust" in its direction. While endeavoring to steady the ship, the crew notice a "little white sugar-loaf hat" hanging from the masthead. Apparently, when the goblin wished to influence a ship's destiny, he'd throw his hat over the ship's mast. The crew, wrote Irving, wouldn't dare to remove the hat, which would remain in place until the ship had left the goblin's terrain.

According to Irving's purported "legend," the goblin king's power had a clearly circumscribed domain ranging from Dunderberg Mountain in the south to Bannerman Island (then called Pollepel) in the north. Beyond this, the king's power subsided. It was said that when old Dutch sailors reached Bannerman, they'd breathe a sigh of relief and watch as the goblin's hat flew high into the air, heading back toward Dunderberg and its rightful owner. In anticipation of their deliverance, they'd tip their hats to the goblin and lower their sails. Or they'd nail an iron horseshoe to the mast as a charm against the goblin's power. (Like the Irish fairies we met earlier in this book, Dutch goblins also hate that potent metal.)

Since Irving introduced the Heer of Dunderberg to his rapt audience in 1822, the goblin has become an ever-present figure of Hudson Valley folklore. The extent to which he's considered an authentic Dutch creation, dated to the era of Dutch colonialism, is testament to the power of Irving's words. More impressive still, the goblin king isn't the only goblin to have sprung fully formed from Irving's pen into Hudson Valley folklore: as we saw in the quote from "The Storm-Ship," the goblin commanded a whole "crew of little imps," commonly known as "ghost imps." Whenever the storm winds raged over the river, it was said that these imps tumbled "head-over-heels" in the air, bringing about the "accidents that so often befall the river craft in the highlands." Apparently representing personifications of the Highlands' weather patterns for Irving, they too, like their king, gradually entered into the realm of folklore, readers interpreting Irving's portrayal as echoing ancient Dutch traditions.

Within about fifty years of Irving publishing "The Storm-Ship," the legend found in the story was so well known among the folk of the Hudson Valley that one anonymous author could call it "*the* legend of the early settlers" and a story "still…repeated in the long winter evenings." The enthusiasm of nineteenth-century folklorists such as Charles Skinner, who wished to populate America's landscape with fairy denizens, further encouraged this tendency to interpret Irving as transmitting authentic legends. Skinner himself informed his readers in 1896 (a full three-quarters of a century after Irving published "The Storm-Ship") that Dunderberg was "chiefly populated by a crew of imps of stout circumference, whose leader, the Heer, is a bulbous goblin."

The ruins of Bannerman Castle on Bannerman Island, where goblins reportedly come out at night. *Author's photo.*

Nowhere is the phenomenon of literature becoming folklore more evident, however, than on tiny, wooded Bannerman Island at the "northern gate" of the Hudson Highlands, where, even today, goblins are said to haunt the Bannerman Castle ruins.

Built in 1901 as a weapons arsenal for the island's owner, Francis Bannerman VI, Bannerman Castle stood proudly on the island's shore until the 1950s, when it was abandoned and fell into disrepair. It's now the perfect gothic home for a swarm of nasty goblins, its moldering walls providing numerous eerie hiding places in which the fairy kind might dwell. Rumors of the ruins' fairy inhabitants have inspired countless tourists to enquire about "Bannerman Island's goblin problem," so much so that the island's Facebook page once responded with the following humorous message: "We haven't seen a goblin there during the day in forever." The implication, of course, is that all bets are off at night.

Legend suggests that over the years, Bannerman became the site of superstitious sailing rituals designed to shield people from the goblins' power. According to historians Thom Johnson and Barbara Gottlock, these rituals included dunking "newer sailors" in the waters around the island to "immunize" them against the Heer's "wrath" before making the journey south.

Of course, the enduring question that hangs over many of these tales is how much of the folklore has genuine Dutch roots and how much should be placed solely at Irving's door.

While it's likely that most recent stories about goblins are attributable to fascination with Irving's work, definite precedent exists in Dutch folklore for many of Irving's ideas. I'll mention a few of them here.

One figure commonly found in Dutch folktales is the goblin king who, like the Heer of Dunderberg, resides inside or under a mountain and rules over an army of goblins and kabouters. Unlike the Heer of Dunderberg and his army of imps, however, the traditional goblin king was associated with the earth and mining, his fairy subjects working on seams of gold deep within the mountain. The Heer's association with the elements of air and water is a novelty that Irving most likely introduced into the traditional Dutch folktale.

Besides the figure of the goblin king, precedent also exists in Dutch folktales for goblins causing mayhem in the lives of humans. In the Dutch material, however, they behave rather differently than Irving's goblins. Called *aardmannetjes* (a Dutch word meaning "little men of earth"), traditional Dutch goblins entered human homes through tiny cracks, wore red caps that made them invisible, stole small children and lived underground. One

Left: Depiction of a Dutch goblin in William Elliot Griffis's *Dutch Fairy Tales for Young Folks* (1918). *Public domain.*

Opposite: Depiction of a Klabautermann, possible inspiration for the Heer of Dunderberg, in *Buch zur See* (1885). *Public domain.*

characteristic of the true Dutch goblin that's consistent with the goblins found on Bannerman Island is that the former only come out at night; goblins in traditional Dutch tales never come out during the day because the sunlight turns them to stone.

Another Northern European fairy that may have inspired Irving's portrayal of the goblin king is the seafaring kobold known in Germany as the *Klabautermann*. According to sailing folklore, ships' captains in the North and Baltic Sea looked favorably on the Klabautermann because they believed that if one inhabited their ship, it would always be kept nice and clean. Unlike the Heer of Dunderberg, the sea kobold was a friendly goblin, sometimes saving a ship's crew from perishing when the vessel was about to sink. The kobold achieved this by making noises amid the rigging and the sails. If the kobold was in a bad mood, however, he'd throw firewood, bang on the sides of the ship or give sailors a blow to the head. While these disruptive behaviors do resemble those of the Dunderberg goblin, a ship usually only ran into trouble in the European context when

the Klabautermann abandoned it. This differs from the story of the Heer, who endangered a ship by sitting on it.

Based on these Dutch tales, it's likely that the inhabitants of New Netherland were indeed familiar with goblin stories, including stories about mountain kings and kobolds. However, it's unlikely they told these stories in quite the same way as Irving. While Irving's stories incorporated the flavor of Dutch folk tales, he wasn't afraid to innovate: his goblin king and army of imps are quite different from the beings he may have learned about from New York's Dutch residents.

THE HOBGOBLIN IN THE CHURCH STEEPLE

To walk the streets of Kingston, New York, with its colonial-era homes and Dutch-style facades, is to experience firsthand the old-world magic that inspired Washington Irving to compose his tales of mischievous goblins and gnomes. Those who visit Kingston for a taste of Irving's Hudson Valley often come prepared to learn about the history of New York's first capital city, but rarely do they expect to come face to face with a supernatural being. Nevertheless, if a certain nineteenth-century legend is to be believed, one of Irving's mythical creations does indeed reside here—trapped in one of the town's old spires.

Believe it or not, nineteenth-century New York State was home, incredibly, to not one but two hobgoblins. We already met the first: it lived in the isolation hole at Fort Niagara at the mouth of the Niagara River. The second, which we're about to meet, lived (or perhaps *still* lives) in the 225-foot-high steeple of Kingston's Old Dutch Church, forty miles north of Bannerman Island. Before we get into that story, we ought to remind ourselves what a hobgoblin is: it's basically the same thing as a goblin (that is, a small humanoid spirit that usually lives underground) but with the prefix *hob* placed before its name.

What does this prefix have to do with the meaning of the word *goblin*?

As I alluded to in the section on Fort Niagara's hobgoblin, the word *hob* in medieval and early modern England referred to a household spirit that either played harmful pranks or performed domestic chores. We might conclude, based on this, that a hobgoblin is a type of goblin that lives around human habitations, meaning it's more likely to interact regularly with people. History's most famous hobgoblin is the English fairy Robin Goodfellow, who often consorted with humans, pranking them or doing them favors.

So how did the hobgoblin of the Old Dutch Church in Kingston end up stuck in the church's steeple? You'll probably be familiar with the story because it has obvious roots in Washington Irving's "The Storm-Ship" and his depiction of the goblin king of Dunderberg.

One day, a Dutch pastor (called a *dominie*) was sailing with his wife alongside the Dunderberg when a hobgoblin landed on the foremast of their ship, causing strong winds to rock the boat uncontrollably. The dominie said a few prayers of deliverance, forcing the hobgoblin to fly forty miles north to Kingston, where his hat became snared on the spire of the Dutch Church's steeple. While attempting to retrieve his hat, he became, according to historian James Werner, "somehow incarcerated in the steeple," and he's been there ever since. Based on one legend that suggests the goblin will remain trapped in the steeple for as long as the church stands on consecrated land, it's possible the hobgoblin took shelter in the building, not realizing the location's sacred nature would trap him there indefinitely.

As you can see, the tale of Kingston's real-life hobgoblin is almost identical to the story of the pastor from Esopus who exorcised the goblin in "The Storm-Ship." The only difference is the location of the church spire where the goblin or hobgoblin's hat became snared. In the early nineteenth century, when Irving wrote his story, churches existed in both Kingston and Esopus. The Kingston church later surpassed the fame of the Esopus church because of its unusually high steeple and classical design, making it one of the most significant historical buildings in the Hudson Valley. Whoever came up with the story of Kingston's hobgoblin must have taken the events mentioned in "The Storm-Ship" and swapped the Esopus church for the more celebrated Kingston one.

Steeple of the Old Dutch Church in Kingston. The clock face bears the numerals XIII in place of XII. *Author's photo.*

The staff at the Kingston church, apparently wishing to stress the church's relevance to the modern world, seem keen to downplay the hobgoblin legend, with one church elder claiming in 2013 that the tale is an "eighteenth-century superstition." The elder may have been a bit off with the dates here, because the first hobgoblin-related event actually occurred in 1870, when the church's present structure was relatively new. The hobgoblin was said to have made faces through the steeple's windows at a man painting the exterior of the church. They say the man died of fright. (For the record, he actually died at the foot of the steeple after succumbing to lead poisoning—from the paint.)

After this event, a series of occurrences took place that suggest the hobgoblin continued to haunt the church throughout the twentieth century. In 1952, church members told a local newspaper that a tavern, which stood opposite the church, offered the best view of the hobgoblin in the town. Unfortunately, the tavern no longer stands.

In 1983, a painter climbing scaffolding around the steeple claimed that he felt the hobgoblin tapping him on the shoulder three times. When he turned around, nobody was there.

More recently, a local historian called James Werner claimed that "old local newspapers" contain reports of individuals seeing the hobgoblin clinging to the steeple during lightning storms; the mischievous fairy is described as being "hard at work" painting the exterior.

Finally, in the 1980s, the historian Pat Murphy claimed that the face of the steeple's clock was believed to have undergone an unnatural change, the Roman numeral XII changing to the unlucky XIII (thirteen). Having visited the church in summer 2024, I can confirm that the clock face does indeed have an extra numeral where the XII should be. "They say the goblin changed [it]," said Murphy.

Now that we've heard the story of the Kingston hobgoblin, perhaps we can venture an explanation as to why the frightening being is called a hobgoblin rather than a goblin (like the Heer of Dunderberg). One possible explanation is that when the mountain-dwelling goblin came to live in the Kingston Church steeple, it could no longer be called a goblin because it now resided in a building frequented by people. Based on our earlier definition of a hobgoblin as a household spirit, we might conclude that the erstwhile goblin of the Hudson Valley Highlands had been domesticated. As a result, it seems only proper that the being should be called a hobgoblin, for the hobgoblin is a type of domestic spirit. Rather than shouting orders at the imps of the wind and rain, this hobgoblin can be heard snoring during church services—a sure sign of its domestication.

One final thought: Perhaps we ought to pray that the hobgoblin remains a hobgoblin. If the church is ever deconsecrated, the being might revert to its true goblin nature, and then all hell would break loose!

THE WHITE LADY AND THE DWARF

For 250 years, the Van Rensselaers, a wealthy Dutch family, owned a property north of Albany that went through many iterations—farmhouse, Georgian mansion, abandoned wreck—before becoming the stuff of legend as a site of fairy hauntings. In its final guise in the late nineteenth century, the property in question was an opulent mansion complete with hand-painted English wallpaper, carved woodwork and the largest entrance hall in North America. When industry expanded into Albany, spoiling the once beautiful town, the Van Rensselaer family abandoned its former seat, and the mansion stood empty for several years before being torn down. As for the Van Rensselaers themselves, throughout their time in the mansion, they reigned over what amounted to a personal kingdom (more accurately, a "patroonship") in eastern New York, becoming famous for mercantile, political and military influence. The fame of their name and of their venerable home was such that while the building stood abandoned in the 1870s and 1880s, and even after it was dismantled in 1895, it continued to cast a legendary spell over the Hudson Valley and its Highlands.

The Van Rensselaer Mansion, legendary home of a dwarf and white lady, photographed in 1890 by Albion W. Floyd. *Public domain.*

The story of the mansion's hauntings—on which its legendary reputation partly rests—came to the attention of folklorists in 1945 when Florence Wojtal, daughter of first-generation Polish American Edward Wojtal, shared a story that her father had told her about a nighttime excursion he took to the mansion when he was still a young man. Florence claimed that a "beautiful white lady" haunted the mansion and that every night around midnight, she could be seen descending the building's grand staircase. Determined to see the specter with his own eyes, Florence's father, Edward, gathered a group of young friends and visited the mansion in the dead of night. What happened next wasn't quite what he expected.

While waiting in the "long grasses" around the neglected building, Edward felt a "sharp tap" on his shoulder. When he turned around, he saw a "dwarf with a long white beard and a red cocked hat." The dwarf looked at Edward and his friends with a "face so ominously cruel in the moonlight" that the men took flight. For a while they waited, breathless, at the edge of the property, and then, when they were sure that the dwarf hadn't followed them, they returned to their spot in the grass. The dwarf being nowhere in sight, they waited for the white lady to appear.

Before returning to our story, I should point out that Florence's description of the dwarf clearly matches elements of Dutch fairy folklore. This is somewhat surprising, because Florence and her father were Polish, not Dutch, and their only connection to Dutch culture was the fact that they resided on old Van Rensselaer land. Either Florence and Edward were familiar with Dutch folklore or the story of the dwarf had long-standing roots in the folklore of Albany, possibly deriving from the city's former Dutch culture.

Indeed, the dwarf's appearance strongly resembles a gnome-like being that the Dutch called a *kabouter*. Nicknamed *redcaps* for the red hats they wore—a trait they shared with other Northern European gnomes and goblins—kabouters resided in caverns and hills and performed good deeds for those who left them offerings of bread and milk. As to why a Dutch kabouter should occupy a colonial-era New York mansion, it makes perfect sense: in Dutch folklore, kabouters often lived close to human settlements, making their homes in nearby caverns. This is because kabouters were friendly beings and only occasionally had a hostile nature.

Although the dwarf in Florence's tale has a cruel-looking face, it's possible that the being's unfriendliness merely arose from a desire to protect the mansion. The dwarf may even have been a *genius loci* or guardian spirit of the place. Although the dwarves of Northern European folklore

Depiction of two kabouters in William Elliot Griffis's *Dutch Fairy Tales for Young Folks* (1918). *Public domain.*

normally worked in mines, fairy-folklore historian Claude Lecouteux has suggested that over the course of history, they gradually transformed into protective spirits or genius loci. Lecouteux claimed that during the medieval era, dwarves underwent a transformation from malevolent spirits to "sympathetic and benevolent [individuals] of the sort…we often encounter in the tales and legends." The latest incarnation of this "friendly dwarf" was the garden-gnome lawn ornament found outside family homes. The dwarf in the Van Rensselaer story does, in fact, resemble one of those whimsical, decorative figures.

Did the Van Rensselaers, when they abandoned their family seat, leave behind a domesticated Dutch kabouter that continued to protect the property from intruders? Based on the tale and its historical context, it's certainly a possibility.

Returning to our story of the white lady, I'll continue (and end) the tale of Edward's spectral encounter with the following quote:

> *Just then one of the boys read his watch in the clear moonlight. It was practically midnight. My father and one of the boys took their stand at one window, while the others clustered about another. For a long time they peered into the inner darkness of the house. Nothing moved. A long shaft of moonlight played directly into the hall and lit up the ancient staircase. They waited tensely. Then suddenly one of the boys gasped. There at the head of the stairs stood a woman in white! Her arms were heavy with chains, chains that were long and dragged after her. Slowly, majestically the white figure descended the stairs. Midway, the figure stopped and appeared to be aware of someone else in the house. Then it resumed its descent more quickly. As it reached the foot of the stairs, it suddenly vanished! And so did my father and the others!*

Based on Florence's description of the "white figure" appearing at midnight with rattling chains, the lady of the Van Rensselaer Mansion appears to be a stereotypical ghost. Indeed, the figure has generally been interpreted in the light of ghostly folklore, her actions suggesting a replay of events that occurred when she was alive, including noticing "someone else in the house" (perhaps her killer?) and descending the stairs more quickly, as if in flight. However, based on the location's Dutch history and the presence of another figure from Dutch folklore outside the house, the story's ghostly trappings may have been a later addition to a more authentically Dutch original. In every other way, the woman resembles those classical figures of

Dutch folklore known as the White Ladies or White Maidens (*Witte Wieven* or *Witte Juffers* in Dutch).

The Witte Wieven were wise women who always appeared in white. Similar to ghosts and sometimes conflated with the dead, they were also associated with supernatural beings such as elves. Like fairies, they lived apart from human settlements in caverns entered via holes in the tops of hills. One popular Dutch folktale describes them as residing in a "deep pit" (called the White Women's Pit) at the top of a hill outside the town of Lochem in the eastern Netherlands. The citizens of Lochem regarded the women as spirits who ought to be left alone. One woman warned her son, "Don't go anywhere near that pit, my boy. These White Women do not want to be disturbed." As for the White Maidens or Witte Juffers, these were even more threatening, often abducting children and adults and taking them down to their underground lair, where they'd later be heard sobbing and wailing.

Although we can never be sure, it seems to me that the story of the Van Rensselaer Mansion's white lady could have originated in a Dutch tale about one of the Witte Wieven before being transformed over time into a ghost story more recognizable to an American audience. The story of a white lady ghost with rattling chains who acts out events from her life before vanishing is certainly more consistent with nineteenth-century ghost lore and the era of spiritualism. Nevertheless, the white lady's name, her ethereal appearance and the fact that she manifested on Dutch-owned land all suggest she could originally have been an elven figure similar, perhaps, to the Witte Wieven. It's likely that any nineteenth- or twentieth-century American storyteller who heard a tale about the Witte Wieven, lacking knowledge of Dutch folklore, would have interpreted the story through the lens of American ghost lore; if the hearer decided to retell the tale, any signs of the woman's ambiguous nature would be lost. I'll leave it up to the reader to decide if the white lady of Van Rensselaer Mansion was a ghost or fairy spirit.

Before putting the Van Rensselaer Mansion behind us, I ought to mention that a particularly thorny problem exists in the story as told by Florence Wojtal. Based on Florence's memory of her father's words, Edward must have visited the mansion sometime in the 1920s, when he was still a young man. But the mansion was dismantled in 1895! Edward Wojtal wasn't born until 1897, so there's no way he could have visited the mansion at all. How can we square Florence's claims with recorded historical facts?

It's possible that Florence got the story wrong and that it was actually her grandfather or an uncle who saw the dwarf and the white lady. It seems unlikely, though, that she'd get such an important detail wrong, especially

Print used in 1660 by historian Johan Picardt to illustrate the type of mound in which the Witte Wieven lived. *Public domain.*

when her father lived for a long time after the events depicted and would have had plenty of opportunities to correct her. Perhaps her father was referring to some other Van Rensselaer mansion. Other old houses in New York do bear the Van Rensselaer name, but none of them is particularly legendary. In fact, it seems highly unlikely that Florence, when evoking the family's name, could have been referring to anything other than the main Van Rensselaer Mansion.

What can we conclude about the story and its discrepancies? Is there a grain of truth lost amid a sea of misremembering and inaccuracies? Or did Florence invent the tale herself, possibly inspired by stories she'd heard in Albany? I can honestly say, perhaps unhelpfully, *I'm not sure.*

CATSKILL GNOMES

Those who've heard thunder rumbling in the sky on a perfectly clear day in the Catskills must surely know that Henry Hudson's men are at their game of ninepins, as described in Washington Irving's "Rip Van Winkle." Those who've passed the mountains in the morning when the hilltops gleam with the rising sun and misty fingers caress the slopes must also know that the fairies have made their homes here, as they have in Irving's writings. Those lucky enough to have visited while actually reading Irving, as I did, must know, too, that the Catskills in real life are equally as beautiful as they are in that author's pages.

A curious mixture of Dutch, Indigenous and English folklore has taken root in these hills, in no small part due to Irving's writings, particularly the seasoning of his tales with mysterious bits of lore. In fact, the power with which Irving evoked the Catskills in "Rip Van Winkle" means it's often difficult to separate history from folklore and folklore from fiction. As Justine L. Hommel, president of the Mountain Top Historical Society, claimed in 1988, "Whether Washington Irving drew the character of Rip Van Winkle from the intrinsic nature of the mountains or whether the Catskill Mountains acquired the personality is irrelevant. What is clear is that the arrival of Rip Van Winkle established the spirit of the Catskill Mountains firmly in the American imagination."

For those unfamiliar with the story, here's a quick recap:

Rip Van Winkle was a lazy but kindhearted man who lived in a village along the Hudson River in the age of King George III. Although Irving

N.C. Wyeth's illustration of the gnome-like men of the Catskill Mountains playing ninepins (1921). *Public domain.*

doesn't name Rip's village in the story, local residents of Leeds, Catskill and Palenville have all since claimed him as a former resident. When Irving's tale began (the author doesn't provide a date), the American colonists were still loyal to the British king, their revolutionary fervor remaining localized in progressive cities like Boston. Partly to escape his nagging wife and partly to indulge his love of nature, Rip spent most of his days outdoors, hiking in the wilderness near his home. It was on one such jaunt in the mountains that he heard a voice calling out to him, "Rip Van Winkle, Rip Van Winkle!"

Turning around, Rip spied a strange-looking man carrying a "stout keg" up the mountainside. The man—"a short, square-built old fellow, with thick bushy hair and grizzled beard"—wore clothes "of the antique Dutch fashion," including a jerkin with "ample" breeches, decorated "with rows of buttons down the side." Rip helped the man carry the keg up the mountain until they came to a natural "amphitheatre" of rock where Rip saw a "company of odd-looking personages playing at nine-pins." All this time, Rip had been hearing what he believed to be thunder roaring among the mountains. He now realized that the sound coincided with the men's bowling balls crashing against the pins.

What does all this have to do with fairies? Well, it was the sight of the men that puzzled Rip, for in every respect, they resembled a group of Dutch gnomes—similar, perhaps, to those kabouters we learned about earlier: "They were dressed in a quaint outlandish fashion: some wore short doublets, others jerkins, with long knives in their belts, and most of them had enormous breeches." It was their "visages," however, that gave away their otherworldly nature, for, as Irving writes, they were extremely "peculiar":

> *One had a large head, broad face, and small piggish eyes: the face of another seemed to consist entirely of nose, and was surmounted by a white sugar-loaf hat, set off with a little red cock's tail. They all had beards, of various shapes and colors.... What seemed particularly odd to Rip was, that though these folks were evidently amusing themselves, yet they maintained the gravest faces, the most mysterious silence, and were, withal, the most melancholy party of pleasure he had ever witnessed....*
>
> *As Rip and his companion approached them they suddenly desisted from their play, and stared at him with such fixed statue-like gaze, and such strange, uncouth, lack-lustre countenances, that his heart turned within him and his knees smote together.*

When the men had finished their bowling, they partook of some "liquor" from the keg that Rip and his companion had carried up the mountain, Rip serving the liquid in "large flagons." What happened next is the crux of the story, for Rip, seeing that he was unobserved, decided to take some of the liquor for himself. After the first sip, he kept going back again and again until the power of the liquor had quite "overpowered him," "his eyes swam in his head" and he fell into a deep sleep. From this ensued the most famous sleep of all American literature: under the influence of this magical liquor, Rip's sleep lasted a whole twenty years, and when he awoke, the world had irrevocably changed: the American colonists had thrown off the yoke of King George III and established the United States.

When Rip descended from the mountain, he found that his old way of life had been completely transformed, his children were fully grown and the citizens of his town—no longer British subjects—had long ago concluded that Rip had disappeared. When Rip recounted his tale, some believed him, while others doubted, but the oldest Dutch inhabitants "almost universally gave it full credit."

It's only at the end of the story that we learn the news, or rather rumor, that the "uncouth" men with whom Rip had drunk were the transformed spirits of Henry Hudson and his men, the first Europeans to travel up the Hudson River in the pay of the Dutch West India Company. Even "to this day," wrote Irving, the mountains' oldest Dutch inhabitants "never hear a thunder-storm of a summer afternoon about the Kaatskill but they say Hendrick Hudson and his crew are at their game of nine pins."

Although this is where Irving ended his tale, the story of Rip's meeting with the gnomes proved so strange and mysterious that many readers were left wanting more. In particular, the question arose as to why Henry Hudson and his crew resembled doleful gnomes. What could account for such a transformation? Although Irving would later mention the crew's haunting of the Catskills again in his short story "The Storm-Ship," he'd say nothing there about the men's appearance, nor did he offer an explanation in "Rip Van Winkle." In fact, Irving nowhere actually called the men *gnomes*. Instead, it was nineteenth-century illustrators such as Arthur Rackham and N.C. Wyeth, inspired by Irving's strange descriptions, who came to depict them as resembling stunted fairies. As these characters passed into Hudson Valley folklore, readers and folklorists became fascinated by these gnomes and took to embellishing their story.

In 1896, Charles Skinner, famous weaver of American legends, produced perhaps the most celebrated embellishment of Irving's tale when he argued that "Mohican pygmies" must have transformed the *Half Moon*'s crew into gnomes when Hudson returned from his exploration of the Hudson River. According to Skinner's legend, these "pygmies" had encountered Hudson and his men deep in the Catskill Mountains and had taken the men to their magical amphitheater—the same amphitheater in which Rip Van Winkle would later encounter them. The pygmies then invited the crew to partake of their magical liquor, turning them into gnomes.

Interestingly, Skinner identified this amphitheater with a real-world location behind the luxurious New Grand Hotel in Highmount, New York. The pygmies worked there in a mine, he said, and the liquor they drank had the power to transform people into oddly shaped beings like themselves:

> [The amphitheater] *is held to be the place of which the Mohicans spoke when they told of people who worked in metals, and had bushy beards and eyes like pigs. From the smoke of their forges, in autumn, came the haze of Indian summer; and when the moon was full, it was their custom to assemble on the edge of a precipice above the hollow and dance and caper until the night was nigh worn away. They brewed a liquor that had the effect of shortening the bodies and swelling the heads of all who drank it, and when Hudson and his crew visited the mountains, the pygmies held a carousel in his honor and invited him to drink their liquor. The crew went away, shrunken and distorted by the magic distillation, and thus it was that Rip Van Winkle found them on the eve of his famous sleep.*

The legend Skinner describes here is a curious fusion of Indigenous folklore about Little People and Dutch-inspired legends from Irving. Although he clearly wished to anchor the legend in Indigenous tales, his description of the "pygmies" and their occupation isn't consistent with Native American folklore about Little People. Although Indigenous Little People do indeed play on the edges of precipices, they never have "bushy beards" and aren't known to work in metallurgy. The legend clearly relies far more on European lore about mining gnomes and fairies.

The story of Rip and Hudson's experience in the mountains, far from representing a meeting with Mohican pygmies, was actually inspired by European descriptions of human dalliances in fairyland. In European tales, people who ventured into the fairies' lair often found that when they returned, many decades had passed—just as Rip did when he awoke from his sleep. If a human ate the fairies' food, he'd even become trapped in fairyland forever—similar to Rip's taking of the magical liquor, for which he

View of the Catskills from the foot of Monka Hill Mountain, site of the gnomes' magical amphitheater, according to Charles Skinner. *Author's photo.*

paid with twenty years. Either that or the fairies would completely transform him, turning him, like Hudson, into a fairy or gnome.

So if Hudson and his men became gnomes in the Catskills, why did they wear such "lack-lustre" expressions? Skinner had an answer for this too, for he clearly distinguished between the Indigenous pygmies of the Catskills and those who became gnomes only after drinking the pygmies' liquor: the Mohican pygmies were happy gnomes who "danced and capered" in the night, whereas Hudson's men—made into gnomes against their will—wore the "gravest faces." It was the latter "ghostly revelers" who could be seen bowling at the back of the New Grand Hotel every twenty years in September when they gathered to drink their mystical moonshine.

As for the magical amphitheater's real-world location, nobody knows exactly when or why it was first identified with the area behind the New Grand Hotel. It's possible that the identification occurred even earlier than 1896 when Skinner wrote his legend. The hotel's insertion into the tale most likely derived from people's eagerness to locate Irving's stories in real-world places. Perhaps readers picked the slope of Monka Hill Mountain behind the hotel as a suitable-looking location, and Skinner followed suit. The hotel's owners may even have encouraged their property's identification with the amphitheater as a way to draw tourists in summer; they wouldn't have been the first to capitalize on Irving's legends.

Writer Edward Wozniak of the *Balladeer's Blog* website offers additional information about the gnomes' dangerous liquor, claiming that it's made from "mountain spring water" given mystical properties by the "submersion of an ingot of the gnomes' mystic metal in each tub of the beverage." Although Wozniak's claim isn't historically attested, it's certainly a pleasing expansion of the Catskill gnomes' folklore.

The hotel where the gnomes gathered to drink their liquor no longer stands, unfortunately. The mountainous location remains, of course, although I haven't been able to find the mystical amphitheater. The next time these gnomes are expected to appear is 2029. So if you're vacationing in Highmount in September of that year, beware of little men offering liquor.

Chapter 3

HAUDENOSAUNEE AND LENAPE LITTLE PEOPLE

The oldest and most elaborate fairy folklore in New York State belongs to the six nations of the Haudenosaunee Confederacy. Commonly known to outsiders as the Iroquois people, the Haudenosaunee were originally five separate peoples occupying land from the Hudson Valley in the east to beyond the Fingers Lakes in the west. These nations (from east to west) are the Mohawk, the Oneida, the Onondaga, the Cayuga and the Seneca. Once upon a time, these neighboring peoples lived in a state of perpetual warfare, but they finally came together in a political union under the direction of Hiawatha and a great prophet called the Peacemaker, thereafter living peacefully side by side. They now share many religious ceremonies and a great deal of folklore about the Little People.

The earliest record of Haudenosaunee belief in the Little People can be found in the 1667 testimony of three Jesuit priests who accompanied a party of Mohawks along the western shore of Lake Champlain (on their way to teach the Christian faith to Mohawk villagers). The priests observed the Mohawk men gathering slabs of flint from the lakeshore and offering tobacco to the underwater-dwelling Little People who they believed had shaped the stones.

Since then, the Haudenosaunee nations have developed diverse traditions about the Little People, a few of which I'll touch on here. Many of these traditions associate the Little People with features of the natural landscape. Oneidan storyteller and clan mother Maisie Shenandoah described the Little People as dwelling "in caves, and in hollow logs, and under rocks," while Cecilia Mitchell, a Mohawk medicine woman, described them as living in the woods and being so small they could "crawl under the weeds." Nineteenth-century Onondaga chief Thomas Webster placed them in a ravine called Gis'-twe-ah-na west of Onondaga Valley, where they liked to slide down the steep clay sides, causing the surfaces to become worn smooth. Ethnologist William Martin Beauchamp identified this "ravine" as Hopper's Glen, a gully with steep sides south of Syracuse. An ancient trail once passed along the edge of the ravine, suggesting that those who traveled the trail may have made offerings to the Little People who lived there.

The Little People are also known to members of the Tuscarora Nation, a tribe that joined the Haudenosaunee Confederacy in 1722, when they settled in western New York's Niagara County. Historically, the Tuscarora called the Little People *ogweshai* (meaning "Little People") and *en-kwe-shu-i-yen* (meaning "not men at all"). The former, according to encyclopedist John Roth, were about two feet tall, spoke in "whoops," wore "fine clothes" and hunted with slings. The latter were about four feet tall, wore fur caps and hunted with bows and arrows.

One fact worth mentioning about the Tuscaroras' relationship with the Little People is that healer Eleazar Williams, born in 1877 on the Tuscarora Reservation, was widely believed to have received his powers from them. According to author Mason Winfield, when Eleazar's father went to work felling trees, he'd leave the boy at a "double-stemmed oak" on a slope where the Little People were known to dwell. As soon as Eleazar's father's wagon had rolled away, "tiny human beings came out, first one, then others, from around the tree, as if they had a door behind it." Many years later, when Eleazar was a man, he'd take his own son, future Tuscaroran medicine man Ted Williams, fishing. According to Ted, the Little People would use their magic to help them catch fish.

The most abundant Little People traditions, however, can be found in the writings of Senecan folklorists such as Arthur C. Parker. Parker identified the home of the Little People as the Genesee River Gorge, a massive crack in the land near the Finger Lakes of western New York. A breathtaking landscape of waterfalls, cliffs and wooded plateaus, the gorge is home to three impressive falls, each providing refuge to a different tribe of Little People. In this chapter, I recount the story of the three tribes, describe the duties assigned to each and explain their relationship to a sacred Senecan ceremony known as the Dark Dance, a ritual in which participants renew their relationship with the Little People and request the healing of a sick tribe member.

Hopper's Glen south of Syracuse. The Little People once enjoyed sliding down the ravine's steep sides. *Author's photo.*

The stories mentioned here are just a few of the many Little People traditions existing among members of the Haudenosaunee Confederacy. In this chapter, I focus mainly on historical folklore and don't attempt to explain contemporary Haudenosaunee attitudes toward the Little People; for that, one would do well to consult Haudenosaunee sources. I should add the following warning, though: according to traditional Haudenosaunee wisdom, summertime storytelling is offensive to the Little People. This is because the summer is a time of activity when animals, plants and humans focus on their natural labors. The winter is a more suitable time for storytelling, according to this logic, because it's quiet and restful. Telling stories in the summer risks causing a cessation of activity, as the plants and animals may turn their ears to the storyteller's words and forget their natural behaviors.

Mabel Powers, an adopted member of the Seneca Nation, learned this the hard way when an old man at a Haudenosaunee council meeting overheard her telling stories in the summer and approached her to explain that he was greatly afraid she might "change into something else right then and there," for it was the habit of the Little People to punish human beings who broke the storytelling taboo. For this reason, it's best not to read these stories out loud in summer or share them with others unless it's winter.

In the second half of this chapter, I introduce the Little People folklore of the Lenape people, an Algonquian tribal nation living today in Ontario, Wisconsin and Oklahoma. Long before the U.S. government's Indian Removal policy forced the remaining Lenape to leave the East Coast, they had for centuries inhabited the forests and wetlands of Manhattan, Long Island and the Hudson Valley. Although they lived quite near to the Haudenosaunee nations, the Lenape were an unrelated people who spoke a dialect of the Algonquian language. Similar to the Haudenosaunee, however, the Lenape believed that Little People inhabited the inaccessible swamps and forests of their homeland. In this chapter, I summarize Lenape traditions about the Little People recorded by those who carried their folklore with them from the eastern United States to Oklahoma and Ontario.

THE VALLEY OF THE THREE FALLS

According to an ancient legend of the Seneca people who inhabit western New York, three tribes of Little People live behind the waterfalls formed by the Genesee River as it flows through a deep gorge in Letchworth State Park, one of New York's most beautiful natural formations. The Seneca call the gorge Seh-ga-hun-da, meaning "the valley of three falls"—a reference to the spectacular waterfalls at the southern end of the park. It's also called the *valley of rainbows*, for rainbows often form in the air when the sun shines through the waterfalls' mists. The falls today are among the most spectacular sights of Letchworth State Park and are intimately associated with the Little People. It's unlikely you'll see one of those magical beings, however (they prefer to remain invisible), and it's best not to mention them unless it's winter.

The creator god of the Seneca, Hawwenio, created the Little People in a primordial time when the world was young and hid them behind the falls of the Genesee River Gorge. For many centuries, they lived apart from humans in the gorge's woods and falls or, according to other sources, in a mysterious place called the "rim of the world," ten days' journey from Haudenosaunee territory. Throughout this time, the Little People wished to make contact with the Seneca, but they were unable to do so because of the great distance. Their first meeting with the Haudenosaunee—recorded in the 1930s by Jesse Cornplanter, a Seneca faithkeeper—occurred in the following way.

Many years ago, when the Seneca lived in close contact with nature and could "converse with animals," a young boy lived with his grandmother in a lodge at the edge of a village. One day, the boy strayed far from his home chasing a black squirrel that he'd wounded with his bow and arrow. The boy and the squirrel had arrived at a tall tree growing out of a deep ravine where the boy could hear high-pitched voices coming from below. When he peered into the ravine, he saw two tiny figures each holding a bow and arrow. Despite the figures' tiny size, the boy recognized them as young boys like himself and could even understand what they were saying: they were discussing the black squirrel perched in the treetop, calling it "the most desired of all meat." Seeing how much the boys wanted it, the Seneca boy drew his bow and shot the creature through the heart, causing it to fall down dead at the boys' feet. Looking up, the Little People spied the Seneca boy watching them from the cliff top and called him down into the ravine to thank him. The boy climbed down onto the forest floor, where he picked up the squirrel and helped the Little People carry it back to their home in one of the ravine's many caves. It was there that he met the boys' mother and father, who fed him corn soup out of a pot that never seemed to empty.

After that, the boy remained with the Little People for many days, learning all about their way of life. The father told the boy to listen carefully to everything he heard so that when he returned to his tribe, he could educate the Seneca in the ways of the Little People, something they'd been longing to do for some time. The boy learned that they were called Jongeoh (Jungies for short) and that they carved their cities out of rock, sometimes tending beautiful gardens in caves. They spent a lot of time hunting the black squirrel and the tiny chickadee, usually going about naked or in dyed deerskins. Most importantly, they were divided into three tribes, each tribe living behind one of the Genesee River Gorge's three great falls. The following is what the boy learned about the three tribes of the Little People.

The Stone Throwers

The first tribe—called Stone Throwers or Gahonga—lived near the entrance of the gorge at a place called Het-ge-oh, which we now call the Upper Falls. These Little People were very strong, capable of uprooting giant trees, and were known to entertain themselves by bouncing off rocks and throwing great boulders. When Hawwenio created the Gahonga, he tasked them with making stone hammers, which he instructed them to leave beside rivers for the Haudenosaunee to find. According to Oneida folklore, if a man or woman required a hammer or corn crusher, he or she would leave sacred tobacco under a stone beside a river (all the Little People love tobacco), and the next day, they'd find a tool left for them by a Stone Thrower.

Evidence suggests that the Stone Throwers were the tribe of Little People that the Haudenosaunee encountered most often. One Stone Thrower sighting comes to us from 1899, when an Onondaga minister, Thomas La Fort, told ethnologist William Beauchamp that he'd seen one about thirty years before when he was "traveling on the road to Albany." He described the little man as sitting on the top of a hill and looking down on the road.

A more detailed encounter comes to us from Mohawk elder and storyteller Josephine Horne, who told of a young girl called Gathering Flowers encountering a family of Stone Throwers after falling asleep beside a river. When the girl awoke, she found herself surrounded by Little People, including a mother, father, three young children and a baby on a cradleboard. Remembering her mother's warning to always be nice to the Little People, she gave the family cornbread and water, and they invited her to their home inside a nearby hill. When they arrived at the top of the hill, the father spat on his hands and placed them on the rocky surface, thereby creating a magical opening. Realizing that the Mohawk girl would not be able to fit inside, he spat on his hands once more and placed them on

The Upper Falls in Letchworth State Park, legendary home of the Stone Throwers of Haudenosaunee folklore. *Author's photo.*

her head, shrinking her to the necessary size. Inside was a cave where they gave the girl soup from a pot that never emptied. After that meeting, they allowed the girl to visit them for the rest of the summer, but they made her promise not to tell anyone where they lived. Because she kept her promise, the Stone Throwers gave her three wishes: she wished for a magical pot so her family would never go hungry, the wisdom never to say hurtful words and the ability to see goodness in everyone she met. The Stone Throwers made each of these wishes come true.

The Hunters

The second tribe of Little People were called Ohdanwas or Hunters (sometimes called Underwater Jungies). They lived at a location in the Genesee River Gorge called Ska-ga-dee, known to us today as the Middle Falls. Evidently, the falls were a kind of portal, for the Hunters actually lived deep under the earth, where they constantly tended to the springs and rivers emerging from underground. In this way, they made sure that the earth's waters remained pure and clean for fish to live in and humans to drink.

According to encyclopedist John Roth, the Ohdanwas were about one and a half feet tall, were "dusky or saffron-colored" and had "stalked, luminous, gold-rimmed, or weak eyes sensitive to sunlight." As well as having pointy chins, they were sometimes depicted with "froglike legs" and "large, webbed hands and feet," befitting their underwater nature. They wore clothes made of amber resin, frog-skin breeches, fish-scale armor and snakeskin belts. Clearly semi-aquatic, they were said to live in dense forests and plains beneath the earth where the White Buffalo, a giant, destructive creature, roamed in darkness. These buffalo were always trying to emerge from the earth to live alongside their brown cousins, but this would mean the overthrow of the balance of creation.

The tribe of Hunters maintained the cosmic order by carrying out two main "underworld" functions. First, when the White Buffalo discovered a path to the light, the Ohdanwas fired arrows at the herd to disperse them, making sure they remained trapped beneath the earth. When they did this, they sent a message to the Little People above the earth telling them to display a red cloud in the sky, a signal that the chase for the White Buffalo had begun. Second, when underworld creatures such as venomous snakes attempted to emerge from underground and spread pestilence among the plants and animals of the forest, the Ohdanwas fought and destroyed them. In this way, the Hunters prevented destructive forces from overturning Haudenosaunee civilization.

The Middle Falls in Letchworth State Park, legendary home of the Hunters of Haudenosaunee folklore. *Author's photo.*

One tradition involving the Ohdanwas suggests that groups of them performed watches at "salt licks," that is, land rich in minerals where buffalo and other mammals gathered to lick the earth. The Haudenosaunee were familiar with salt licks because they knew the buffalo would be there when hunting season came. While the Haudenosaunee wished to hunt the buffalo, the Little People's major concern was to guard the salt licks from the White Buffalo that rose up through the mud to escape their underworld pastures. (Regarding these salt licks, the most commonly identified is at present-day Big Bone Lick State Park in Boone County, Kentucky, where mammoth and mastodon fossils have been recovered.)

Besides protecting the world from subterranean monsters, the Hunters also occasionally emerged from underground to hold festivals in the forest and to dance, in Harriet Maxwell Converse's words, in the "circle beneath many a deep wood tree, where the grass refuses to grow." (Of course, they did this only at night, for their eyes couldn't stand the sunlight.) In this way, they were sometimes associated, like European fairies, with "fairy rings," circular patches in the grass where the grass failed to grow.

The Drum Dancers

The third tribe of Little People lived a few miles downriver at the Lower Falls, a curtain of foaming water rather wider than the other falls. These Little People were known as Gandayah or Drum Dancers because, being invisible, the sound of their drumming was the only thing that gave away their presence. These Little People were true nature spirits, for they spent the springtime whispering to the seeds and encouraging them to shoot. In summer, they turned the plants to the light and ripened the hanging fruit.

One of the Drum Dancers' most important functions was to tend to the strawberry plant, which the Haudenosaunee hold sacred, a gift of the Sky Woman when she fell to earth from the Sky World (an event that occurs in the Haudenosaunee creation story). At winter's end, the Drum Dancers loosened the soil around the plant so its shoots could penetrate the earth. When the plant put forth its fruit, the Drum Dancers painted the fruit its characteristic red and protected the plant from insects and mold.

When the leaves lay heavy on the ground and the north wind blew, the Drum Dancers took refuge in the shadows behind the falls and waited for

The Lower Falls in Letchworth State Park, legendary home of the Drum Dancers of Haudenosaunee folklore. *Author's photo.*

the snow to melt and the sun to shine so they could return to their care of the fruits and grains. Others hibernated under fallen leaves.

They also appeared to the Haudenosaunee in the form of birds, taking the form of robins when they wished to bring good fortune, owls when they needed to warn the Haudenosaunee about a deceitful enemy and bats to foretell a struggle to the death.

THE DARK DANCE

After the Seneca boy had learned all about these different tribes, the Little People said he was ready to learn about a sacred dance that they'd long desired to teach to the Seneca. More than anything, the Little People wanted the Seneca to perform this dance as a way to honor and communicate with them. Before the dance began, the mother of the family cooked a pot of corn soup and used a special drum to gather her kin for a great feast. Then, over a series of nights, the Little People taught the boy the sacred dance, which had to take place in darkness and was therefore called the Dark Dance. First came the smoking of sacred tobacco. Then they passed around a strawberry-juice drink. This was followed by an opening speech. The dance then progressed through a series of songs, the Seneca boy listening carefully to each so that when he returned to his Seneca home, he could teach them to the tribe's elders.

The Little People told the boy that when the Seneca performed the Dark Dance, they should burn tobacco as an offering and bang a drum that would call the Little People to the dance from a distance of ten days. The Little People would join the Seneca in the darkened room where the ritual was held, although the Seneca would never see them, only hear the sound of their footsteps or feel the brush of their clothing. Those who performed the Dark Dance would receive a bundle containing powerful animal charms (usually dead parts of a sacred animal), which would grant the bearer luck if they performed the dance correctly. The charm would be passed down from one generation to the next and would always bring the family luck unless they neglected the Little People by failing to perform the ritual; it would then act as a curse, bringing sickness.

Other requirements of those who performed the Dark Dance included making bundles of nail parings and throwing them over cliff tops as offerings to the Little People. The Little People used these bundles to disguise their

Dark Dance of the Little People by Cheyenne artist Walter Richard West Sr. *Courtesy of the National Museum of the American Indian, Smithsonian Institute (23/8382).*

natural smell, making it easier for them to hunt the animals of the forest, especially the black squirrel.

After the Seneca boy had learned all this, the Little People allowed him to return to his people. When he arrived at his village, he found that many years had passed, which to him had seemed like a matter of days. His grandmother was astonished to see him, for everyone had long ago given up hope of ever finding him. In the days that followed, the boy did everything the Little People said: he gathered the tribe for a feast of corn soup and taught them how to perform the Dark Dance ceremony. The ceremony began with an opening speech and the burning of sacred tobacco. When the boy began to sing in the darkness amid the gathered tribe members, they were amazed at how well he could sing. This was because the father of the Little People family had arrived, as promised, and had joined his voice with the boy's, although only the boy knew he was there.

For many years, the Dark Dance ritual was a well-kept secret among the Seneca. The tribe members who practiced the ritual became known as a secret medicine society, their ceremony, like other medicine-society ceremonies, forming part of traditional Senecan religion. For many years, these societies were so secretive that anthropologists outside the Seneca

Nation began to question whether they even existed. However, in 1936, Jesse Cornplanter explained that he had inherited the "obligation" to perform the Dark Dance from his great-grandfather Henry Phillips, a veteran of the War of 1812. This Henry Phillips had possessed an animal charm that required him to perform the dance. Cornplanter described himself as the latest "victim" of the charm and said he needed to perform the dance to break the charm's "spell." Doing this kept him and his family healthy and in good fortune.

The outside world learned more about the Dark Dance ceremony in 1958, when representatives of the Seneca Nation invited the writer Edmund Wilson to visit their Allegany Reservation and observe the ritual of the Dark Dance in person. This caused controversy at first: not all the participants were in favor of allowing a non-Senecan man to observe their ceremonies, but they eventually agreed to allow it. Wilson described the ceremony as taking place in a "very large kitchen" of a private home rather than the communal longhouse where most ceremonies took place. This is because medicine-society dances don't pertain to the entire tribe; they involve only members inducted into the ritual—for instance, through being healed.

Wilson arrived late at the dance and missed the first song, but upon arriving, he saw that an elderly woman had cooked a giant pot of corn

Jesse Cornplanter's sketch of the Dark Dance Ceremony, found in H.M. Converse's *Myths and Legends of the New York Iroquois* (1908). *Public domain.*

soup and that musicians and singers had taken seats around the kitchen wall, leaving space in the middle for the dancers to perform. Between each song and dance, the lights of the home were switched on to allow for a short break. In this way, said Wilson, the series of songs produced something of an "oratorio." The sequence began with an invocation to the Little People, drumming and the burning of sacred tobacco, the smoke of the tobacco traveling to the Little People across a distance of ten days' journeying. The invocation began with the admission that a member of the Seneca Nation had fallen sick as a result of the Little People's actions and that the ceremony was intended to return that person to health. This person would then become a member of the Dark Dance Society. Wilson transcribed the invocation as follows:

> *So now you get tobacco—you, the Great Little People.*
> *Now is the time when you have come;*
> *You and the members assembled here tonight.*
> *Now again you receive tobacco—you, the Great Little People.*
> *You are the wanderers of the mountains;*
> *You have promised to hear us whenever the drum sounds,*
> *Even as far away as a ten days' journey.*
> *You well know the members of this society,*
> *So let this* [the illness] *cease.*
> *You are the cause of a person, a member, becoming ill.*
> *Henceforth give good fortune, for she* [or he] *has fulfilled her duty and given you tobacco.*
> *You love tobacco and we remember it;*
> *So also you should remember us.*
> *How the drum receives tobacco,*
> *And the rattle also.*
> *It is our belief that we have said all,*
> *So now we hope that you will help us.*
> *Now these are the words spoken before you all,*
> *You who are gathered here tonight.*
> *So now it is done.*

Wilson went on to describe how the Little People's arrival in the room occurred with the sound of shifting feet, as the visitors stumbled "over [the occupants'] legs." After they'd taken up their positions in the room, the Little People were believed to sing "in their own language, which nobody understands." The fact that the ritual took place in darkness allowed the participants, Wilson wrote, to imagine that "the characters… [were] actually in the room." The effect, he explained, was both "exciting" and "frightening," giving the impression of an "independent existence, embodying some projection of the human spirit which has survived through uncounted centuries." At the end of the Dark Dance ritual, it's believed that the Little People "go back to their rocks, over the hills, beyond the horizon," taking ten days' journey to complete the trek.

Besides learning about the content and structure of the Dark Dance ceremony, Wilson was also able to question the hostess about why she'd decided to organize the ritual. Becoming "silent, sober, and thoughtful" when asked, she explained that her father had regularly hosted the Dark Dance because "he had felt that his family owed the Great Little People a special debt." His uncle, the woman explained, had gone missing once in the woods when he was ten years old and hadn't reappeared for a month. When they found him, he couldn't explain where he'd been, and so the family concluded that the Little People must have taken him "to save him from some threatening misfortune." The family concluded that the Little People had done a great service to them and ought to be properly thanked through regular performances of the Dark Dance. For the woman, the Dark Dance represented "something very ancient which had been…a part of her childhood world and which was difficult to explain to outsiders."

One aspect of the woman's relationship with the Little People deserves particular attention because it confirms what we know about the Little People from other Haudenosaunee sources. Almost all Haudenosaunee folktales about the Little People involve interactions with children, whether the story of Gathering Flowers and her visit to the Stone Throwers or the tale of the boy who met the Little People family in the ravine. Often, in these stories, the Little People teach the child about important matters that they wish to communicate to the tribal elders. In other stories, the Little People reach out to young people, especially orphans, to comfort them. This motif can be seen in a story told by Mabel Powers in which the Little People rescued a poor abused Haudenosaunee girl and took her on a journey in a magical flying canoe (flying canoes are a typical feature of Little People stories).

Another tale involving the Little People's interactions with a child comes to us from Jesse Cornplanter. He explained that long ago when the Seneca lived in union with nature and could converse with animals, a little boy who'd recently learned to hunt went to a local river to look for waterfowl and heard a sudden "swishing noise" coming from upstream. When he looked toward the sound's source, he saw a tiny canoe coming around the river bend at a "rapid speed." The canoe contained "two of the tiniest little men" the boy had ever seen. In no time at all, the little men pulled up to where the boy was standing and disembarked, each carrying a tiny bow and arrow. When they saw the Seneca boy's bow and arrow, they offered to trade it for one of theirs, but the boy told them that their bows were far too small. "That may be true," the little man replied, "but all great things on earth are not always the biggest; you may live to learn that." And with that, the little man drew his tiny bow, looked up into the sky and shot an arrow so high that none of them saw it come down.

According to one version of the story, which differs from Cornplanter's own, the two little men got back into their boat and the boat soared high into the air, disappearing over the nearby treetops. The boy went home and told his grandmother what had happened, and she chided him, saying that he should have accepted the trade because the Little People's bows and arrows were magical, ensuring constant success in hunting. "Hereafter never be too hasty in judging people as you see them," said the grandmother, "for you never know who or what they may be."

LENAPE WOOD DWARVES

When Dutch traders and explorers first moored their sailing ships on the shores of Manhattan in the early seventeenth century, the people they met there, the Lenape, had lived on that island for hundreds of years, hunting and gathering and growing crops such as corn, beans and squash. Manhattan was very hilly then, and the Lenape had settlements in the north and south of the island, where they made their homes out of bark. When hunting season came, they traveled north along a trail that would one day become Broadway. And when they traded with other Native American peoples like the Mohicans and the Haudenosaunee, they used dugout canoes to navigate the Hudson River.

Even before the Europeans arrived in Manhattan and changed their lives forever, the Lenape were never alone in *Lenapehoking* (the name they gave to their homeland), for besides the animals that roamed in the forests, spirits everywhere inhabited the swamps and woodlands that surrounded them. Among these spirits was a mysterious dwarf called *wemategunis* (sometimes called *matekanis*). This dwarf (or class of dwarves, according to some stories) stood waist high to an adult male, was extremely strong and resembled a small brown boy (he was sometimes described as "odd-looking" with a large round belly).

Lenape historian Richard C. Adams described the wemategunis as a messenger of the Great Spirit who appeared to the Lenape during battles with other nations. Legend suggests that in the days before European contact, when the Lenape's traditional ways were strong, every tribe member had the ability to see spirits; hence, they could see the wemategunis deflecting enemy projectiles and guiding the actions of their leaders. In this role, the dwarf tended to wear war gear such as eagle feathers, buckskin leggings and war paint.

When he wasn't helping the Lenape in battle, the wemategunis ruled over the animals of the forest and could be seen riding on the backs of wild deer. In these activities, he served the Lenape spirit Mesingw, the guardian of game animals in Lenape religion. Generally invisible, this mysterious dwarf was nevertheless often extremely friendly, helping hunters who ran into trouble in the woods or occasionally pranking them.

Many years after the European settlers had driven the Lenape from their eastern homelands to territories such as Kansas and Oklahoma, Lenape elders began to record the folklore they'd carried with them from the east, hoping to preserve important cultural traditions for future generations. One storyteller, an elder called Julius Fouts, related a tale about the wemategunis that he'd learned in the late nineteenth century. The tale concerned a Lenape hunter's interactions with a dwarf in the eastern woodlands. I share it here as an example of the type of story that the Lenape may have told about the wemategunis since time immemorial and for the insight it offers into how these magical dwarves interacted with human beings.

In the tale, the hunter was carrying a deer carcass through a woody hollow when he realized that he'd lost his friends. Hoping to locate them, he made a loud "whoop" and waited until he'd heard a call answering from the other side of the hollow. The hunter followed the sound but couldn't find anybody there. Letting out another whoop, he once more followed the answering whoop back across the hollow. All this time he was sweating profusely, for he was still carrying the deer on his back.

Eventually, the hunter came across a hunched-over dwarf wearing a large cornhusk coat. The dwarf had apparently been mocking the hunter the entire time, drawing him back and forth across the hollow.

When the hunter asked the dwarf why he'd led him on a wild goose chase, the dwarf said he wanted to test the hunter's strength and see how far he

A Lenape settlement on Manhattan Island as it may have appeared in the sixteenth century, found in *The Memorial History of New York* (1892). *Public domain.*

could carry the deer. Angrily, the hunter challenged the dwarf to a fight, and the dwarf responded that he must first remove his coat. As soon as the dwarf had done so, the hunter realized that the dwarf was wearing another coat under the first and would have to remove this coat as well. The hunter waited until the dwarf had removed the second coat and realized that a third lay under the second. This interaction continued in much the same way until the dwarf had removed a total of twelve coats, at which point he looked so small that the hunter was ashamed to fight him. In the end, the hunter went away without a fight, telling the dwarf he would name him "Answer-me," a reference to the strange manner in which they'd met.

Based on this rather humorous story, it seems that the wood dwarves of Lenape folklore interacted with human beings to teach them a good lesson, the dwarf wishing to test the hunter's strength. In other tales, the wemategunis gravitated toward Lenape children, reflecting the belief that the Little People sometimes intervened in children's lives to save them when they were lost or befriend them at home. James Webber Witapanoxwe, a Lenape elder who recorded his people's folklore for posterity, has left us with a rich understanding of this aspect of wemategunis behavior. He said that in the old days when the Lenape were "clean" due to their continued practice of the traditional ways, a young boy went to play in the woods and met a dwarf there whom he liked very much. The boy went back to the woods again and again to play with the dwarf until his friends noticed his long absences from home and asked him where he kept going. The boy told them that he'd been visiting a friend in the woods. Soon after this, the boy began to see the dwarf while he was playing with his peers. Although he'd point at the dwarf, none of the other children could see him.

Witapanoxwe explained that according to traditional Lenape wisdom, everybody has the ability to see spiritual beings like the wemategunis, but only a few people actually hone this ability. Those who do receive a vision of the dwarf tend to gain immense strength and hunting prowess as a result of their openness to the spiritual world. In the 1930s, Witapanoxwe said that most Lenape had changed their mode of life to such an extent that very few people could actually see the dwarves. Other sources suggest that if a hunter boasts about his dwarf-given power, he'll lose that power immediately.

Another Lenape story about the Little People comes to us from Kansas long after the Lenape had completed their migration from the eastern woodlands. Although the story was recorded in the Midwest, I share it here because it offers insight into the kinds of ideas about the Little People that later generations of Lenape inherited from their ancestors. According to the testimony of Nora Thompson Dean of Oklahoma, the Little People sometimes took a female form and could even be found inside Lenape dwellings. Nora's mother, Sarah Wilson Thompson, had recently returned from Coffeyville, Kansas, and had opened the door to her home when she saw a group of Little People "scattering" out of sight. Before they vanished, Sarah heard one of the Little People say to another, "My friend, they are home," using a feminine version of the word for *friend*. This implies that one of the Little People was a girl or woman. (It seems significant that the encounter took place in a private home, for this is an unusual feature of Little People stories, the Little People generally preferring to stay outside in the woods.)

Besides Sarah's indoor meeting with the Little People, she also encountered them late one night while attending an "Indian dance." She'd just taken a break from the dancing and had gone into the woods with her cousin when the Little People surrounded them. So many small beings emerged from the trees that Sarah "was afraid to step for fear of stepping on them." Apparently, they spoke the Lenape language, suggesting that they too had migrated west with the Lenape.

One final story involving a wemategunis comes to us from Richard C. Adams. In 1905, he shared a traditional Lenape folktale in which the dwarf makes a memorable appearance. The tale concerned a young Lenape man with beautiful eyes who'd unfortunately devoted himself to gambling and influenced many young men to become involved in the habit. To teach the man a lesson, a spirit called Che-py-yah-poo-thwah, who resided on the moon as the "great chief of the gamblers," came down to earth one day and manipulated the man into gambling away his eyes. When the man had lost the game, the spirit took his eyes back to the moon, saying, "My young friend, if you had made better use of your eyes, you would have them still." In the days that followed, the man moved into a "little bark house" and was "deserted by his friends."

One day, a little boy (who was actually a wemategunis) visited the man and told him that if he promised to make better use of his eyes and never gamble again, he'd go to the moon and win them back for him. Of course, the man agreed, and the dwarf flew hastily to the moon. When he arrived, he saw that an old woman was wearing the man's eyes around her neck like jewels. The dwarf asked if he could see them, and once he had them, nobody was brave enough to take them back. He flew back down to earth and put them back into the man's head, and from that day on, the man never gambled again.

DOLL SPIRITS

In addition to wood dwarves or Little People of the woods, the Lenape believed that spirits could inhabit dolls made from sticks and become attached to individuals and families. These dolls (called Nani'tis in the Munsee Lenape dialect) were usually about eight inches long, had carved faces, wore female clothing and often belonged to women. Some Lenape families were known to pass the dolls from one generation to the next for over one hundred years. It was believed that the spirit dwelling in the doll could hear and see everything in its vicinity and could even become vengeful if mistreated, striking down its owner with sickness. The woman who owned a doll called it the "guardian of health," as well as "mother" and "grandmother," treating the doll with special respect because she believed that her health was intimately tied to the doll's well-being. Every year, the owner was expected to perform what was known as the Doll Dance, in which she fed the doll, gave it new items of clothing and killed a doe for a great feast.

James Wolf, a Lenape resident in Ontario at the beginning of the twentieth century, explained that his mother had possessed a doll that

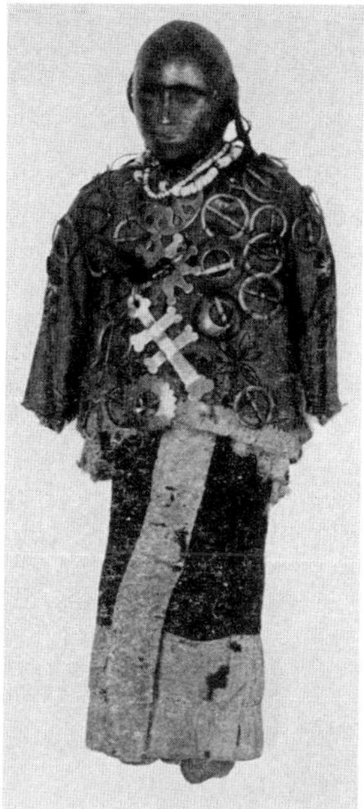

Photograph of a Lenape doll spirit, originally appearing in M.R. Harrington's *Religion and Ceremonies of the Lenape* (1921). *Public domain.*

she treated with religious reverence, always performing the Doll Dance ritual in the fall when the deer were in "their best condition." The mother believed the doll was able to walk about on its own, for she sometimes found the hem of its skirt all worn and soiled, with burrs stuck to it, as if it had been walking in the woods.

Various stories arose among the Lenape to explain the nature of the doll spirits, one of which I share here.

Legend suggests that long ago, a Lenape girl walking in the woods found a stick that resembled a human form. She took it home, dressed it in miniature clothes and kept it as a doll. The girl's parents became alarmed at the way their daughter behaved toward the doll, for she treated it as if it was a real child. As a result, they made her throw it away. Over the next few nights, the girl complained of bad dreams in which the doll appeared to her as a living person, seemingly ready to attack her. Eventually, she fell sick, and an old man told the family that the only way they could restore their daughter to health was to make a doll in which the offended spirit could live. Every year, to please the spirit, they'd have to perform the Doll Dance ceremony and offer the doll food and gifts.

As for the structure of the Doll Dance ceremony, folklorist M.R. Harrington recorded the Munsee Lenape version of it in his *Religion and Ceremonies of the Lenape*. It involved the owner of the doll hiring a man to hunt a "yearling doe," that is, a female deer in its second year. This happened during the fall hunting season. The woman would then hold a feast for any women who wished to attend. A man would beat a small drum, and the women would dance around the room holding the doll. They would then feed the doll and offer it gifts such as new clothing.

Reverence of doll spirits continued among the Lenape well into the nineteenth century. Attitudes then began to change. In 1839, a Presbyterian missionary called Reverend Cutting Marsh wrote an interesting description of a doll when a Christian-convert Lenape man approached him to dispose of one. The "idol," as the man termed it, had long been a possession of his family, and according to Marsh, the man was only too pleased to get rid of it. Of course, Marsh's Christian perspective may have tainted his description of the doll, but I share it here in full nevertheless: "It was indeed…a horribly looking object about the size of a common doll; fantastically arrayed in Indian costume and nearly covered with silver broaches and trinkets; and whilst retained as an object of worship was kept wrapped up in some 20 envelopments of broad-cloth trimmed with scarlet ribbon."

Marsh went on to explain that the doll wasn't an object of "love and compassion" for the family but rather of "fear or dread." Although it's quite likely that Lenape women felt some affection for the dolls, especially in the precolonial era, it's also probable that the Lenape who converted to Christianity in Canada or Wisconsin ended up seeing the dolls in a negative light. One instance of a doll being seen as an object of fear rather than of affection can be found in a folktale told by Martha Ellis of Oklahoma. In Martha's story, an old woman bequeathed a doll to a young woman who did everything she could to get rid of it. Unfortunately, the doll kept returning of its own accord. Eventually, a boy threw the doll away, but soon after, he went mad. The folktale appears to have arisen from a desire to stress the importance of respecting the dolls and performing the proper ritual once a year. Otherwise, the doll could become vengeful.

Perhaps, after all, there was some truth to Reverend Marsh's words.

Chapter 4
MISCELLANEOUS FAIRY STORIES

Previous sections of this book have presented clearly defined bodies of folklore such as Irish or Indigenous tales. These stories were bound together because they belonged to the same community, each story providing additional evidence of fairy belief in the given context. In contrast, this section of the book collects stories that aren't easily categorized, whether because they're few in number or poorly attested. One example of a poorly attested tradition found here is the story of Bill Greenfield's encounter with the Little People in the Adirondack foothills. The story represents a weak tradition because no other stories about Little People can be found in a similar context. I share it here because the obscurity of the story doesn't make it any less fun or interesting from a historical perspective. The Welsh stories in this section (also from the Adirondack foothills) are similarly few in number and rather obscure. I share them here because they may represent a larger body of folklore that's never come to light.

Other not so easily categorized stories featured in this part of the book are the modern-day findings of the Fairy Censuses of 2014–17 and 2017–23. These represent a separate tradition of fairy stories because they don't necessarily belong to a particular ethnic community, as other stories do. They depict fairies in ways that differ markedly from the fairies of earlier folklore, as we'll see. While the rest of this book focuses on historical folklore, this section offers a summary of beliefs found in present-day New York.

LITTLE PEOPLE OF THE ADIRONDACKS

If certain "tall tales" and whispered legends are to be believed, the Adirondack Mountains of northern New York are no less attractive to the Little People than other parts of New York, although the sources here are murkier than elsewhere in the state. The Adirondacks are home to some of the most remote territory in New York, including isolated communities such as the fabled Allentown, a place that resists almost all outside interference (however well-intentioned), so perhaps one might not be too surprised to find that the fairies live here too.

If the Little People do abide in these mountains, it's unlikely that the industrial convulsions of the nineteenth century left their lives untouched. Logging was one of the Adirondacks' most important industries at that time (hemlock bark was particularly valued for its tannins, which were used to create leather). By the 1880s, however, logging had become so intense in areas such as the Sacandaga Valley that the woods were often decimated. Any Little People who resided here couldn't have been happy about the encroachment of human industry on their formerly pristine domain. Besides, for how long could storytellers tell tales about the Little People while busily removing the woods in which they dwelled?

One area of the mountains I'm particularly interested in for the purpose of this book is the southern Adirondack foothills, especially the towns north of the Great Sacandaga Lake such as Northville, Edinburg and Day. The events I'll be covering in this section occurred long before New York State flooded the Sacandaga Valley to create the man-made reservoir we see today. This means that many of the towns that existed then are now covered in water.

It was in this neck of the woods (quite literally) that a man called Bill Greenfield saw the Little People with his own eyes.

Born in 1833, Bill carved out a life for himself as a farmer, logger, trapper and hunter, activities that must have brought him in proximity to any magical beings lurking in the Adirondack woods. In these occupations, Bill took after his father, Abner, and many other farmers and lumbermen who'd migrated to New York from Scotland around the year 1800. However, it wasn't so much Bill's work that made him famous as the outrageous stories he told.

After his death in 1903, Bill became a legendary figure of New York folklore, famous for his intrepid "man of the woods" persona and the tall tales he spun about extraordinary feats such as lifting plows with one bare hand, living with bears for whole seasons at a time and cutting down enormous

Modern-day sketch of Bill Greenfield by artist Tom Trujillo (1991). *Courtesy of Tom Trujillo.*

trees that sometimes stretched from New York to Oregon. These stories circulated widely in the southern Adirondack foothills, particularly in the lumber camps where men spent the winter with little entertainment except exaggerated storytelling. They earned Bill the title of "the goldarndest, most unreasonable liar you ever saw."

(In Saratoga County, where the Greenfield family lived, Bill's father, Abner, was almost as famous for his "lies" as Bill, and there's some debate about whether the events related in Bill's tales originally pertained to Abner. This is based on a statement made by Bill's son Frank, who, long after Bill had died, told researchers in Massachusetts that all the stories Bill told were mere repetitions of stories he'd learned from Abner.)

However far-fetched their stories may have been, Bill and Abner definitely existed in these mountains: their lives are clearly documented. In this, they differ from more famous figures of North American folklore such as the gigantic lumberjack Paul Bunyan, whose historicity is by no means certain. I can also vouch for Bill's existence: in the summer of 2024, I looked for his grave at Clarkville Cemetery near Edinburg and found it positioned (appropriately) beside a logging camp, the mountains creating a fine prospect behind it. On that visit, I met one of Bill's descendants, Priscilla Edwards, who's now a historian in the town of Edinburg, where Bill was born. She assured me that after Bill died in 1903, many generations of Adirondack dwellers faithfully shared his tales and adventures.

But what about Bill Greenfield's encounter with the Adirondack fairies? Well, according to legend, Greenfield saw the Little People on a jaunt in the woods near his home one day and later told his neighbors all about it. The esteemed New York folklorist Louis C. Jones, to whom we're indebted for many of the Irish stories in this book, shared the following whimsical tale about Bill, which he claimed to have picked up from existing Saratoga County folklore (unfortunately, he doesn't provide a source):

> [They] *also tell of Bill that once he was out in the woods logging when he heard tiny voices and when he finally looked around he found the littlest people in the world, a whole family of them living in a quart oyster can. Bill saw a father and two sons bringing in their winter food supply: a single beech nut which they were dragging along with a cant hook, smaller than a hairpin. Bill talked to them for a spell and afterward he reported that, "They were good, smart talking people."*

As you can see, the Little People in this tale are evidently extremely small, for they live inside an oyster can. Their activity appears to mirror the activity of the human beings who live beside them in the woods, for they possess a tiny "cant hook," a type of tool used by loggers to maneuver logs. In the story, the Little People are using the tool to drag a "single beech nut," although it's not entirely clear whether this "beech nut" refers to an *actual* nut or the tree itself (that is, the American beech or beechnut tree). If it's the former, it's likely the Little People were preparing the nut for their winter victuals. If the "beech nut" refers to the tree itself, on the other hand, we're left with the paradoxical impression of tiny men pulling an entire tree with a cant hook the size of a "hairpin." Although this doesn't necessarily defy the logic of the tall tale—such tales often involve impossible events—it's quite unusual for a Bill Greenfield story to feature a meeting with such tiny people. While his stories nearly always involve some exaggerated aspect of Adirondacks life, whether logging, hunting or

Bill Greenfield's grave in Clarkville Cemetery outside the town of Edinburg, including a star for his Civil War service. *Author's photo.*

farming, they never really involve magical or tiny beings. It seems the story requires some extra investigation.

When I asked Priscilla Edwards, Bill's distant relative, whether she'd heard of any Little People stories involving Bill, she said she wasn't aware of a single one. Despite hearing dozens of tales about Bill from her father and grandfather while growing up in the area, she didn't remember hearing anything about the Little People. This puzzled me because Louis Jones, a respected folklorist, had clearly shared the tale and included many precise details that gave it the aura of an authentic folktale. Why, therefore, was the tale not known to the very person you'd think would be most likely to have heard it? The answer may lie in Louis Jones and the source from which he drew.

The only book Jones credits for his knowledge of Bill Greenfield is New York folklorist Harold Thompson's *Body, Boots and Britches*. It was this classic of New York folklore that spread Bill Greenfield's fame beyond Saratoga County and the Adirondack Park when it was published in 1940. There, we find a story (told by a Mr. Peleg Andrew of Corinth, Saratoga County) that shares many features with the Louis Jones story despite being quite different. Told in Bill's voice, the tale reads as follows:

> *While I was passing through the woods one day, I heard a funny sound, and getting nearer I heard a man say, "He-O-He—tuck under!" Soon I come to a small clearing where there was four men and a five gallon keg. Two of the men with levers were trying to turn over a beechnut; the third man had a big wooden wedge, and when they raised the beechnut with the levers and when the fourth man gave the order to tuck under, he pushed the wedge under to hold what they had gained. At last they had the beechnut turned over, and just then a shower came; so the four men all went into the bunghole of the keg.*

It's not entirely clear from the story if the men involved are meant to be understood as little or not. Although they jump through the keg's "bunghole" to escape the rain, this could be a feature of the tall tale genre, which often involves absurd events that defy the laws of physics. As for the fact that the men are trying to turn over a "beechnut," this appears to be a reference to the American beech tree rather than a single nut, which further suggests that the individuals in the story are full-grown men. In this case, the men's "littleness" appears to reside only in the fact that they jump through the keg's bunghole. Did Louis Jones read this story and mistake the word "beechnut" as a reference to an actual *nut*? Combining this with the bunghole incident, he may well have concluded that the story attested to Bill's encounter with the Adirondacks' Little People.

But what of the other features of Jones's tale, such as the Little People's home inside an "oyster can" and their cant hook the size of a hairpin? These details undeniably suggest that the people in the story are *Little People*. Did

Jones, when recalling Peleg Andrew's story, forget the details of the tale and invent his own to fill in the gaps? Or had he genuinely heard a folktale about Bill and the Little People in Saratoga County, forgetting to cite the source? (It may surprise some to learn that an eminent folklorist such as Louis Jones might have altered a traditional tale; however, academic standards differed markedly in the 1940s, so it may well have been the case.)

Whether Little People folklore was ever an aspect of Bill Greenfield stories in the Adirondack Mountains remains a mystery. Priscilla Edwards's lack of familiarity with such stories suggests that, if they did exist, they weren't exactly an important feature of Adirondack lore. For now, I'll simply take pleasure in imagining our famous lumberman strolling through the woods and coming unexpectedly upon the Adirondack equivalent of the fairies: beech tree–logging Little People who live in a quart-sized oyster can. As the descendant of a Scottish farming family, Bill may well have heard stories about the "wee people" back home. Had he discovered that they'd followed his ancestors across the pond?

ANOTHER MURKY BUT FASCINATING tale comes to us from the southwest foothills of the Adirondacks in the vicinity of Remsen and Steuben. Around the same time that Bill Greenfield's Scottish ancestors settled in the Sacandaga Valley—about 1800—Welsh immigrants began to arrive in Oneida County, where they set about deforesting the area to make way for dairy farms. The earliest families to complete the voyage came from the Llyn Peninsula in Caernarfonshire, not far from the fairy-haunted mountains of Snowdonia. As more and more Welsh people arrived throughout the nineteenth century, towns such as Remsen sprang up around log or stone-built chapels where the immigrants held services in their mother tongue. While these early settlers must have been familiar with the fairy folklore of Wales, it's unlikely they professed a belief in fairies or talked about them much. That's because they were deeply religious Christians of the Baptist, Congregationalist and Methodist stripe. When they arrived on these shores, they were deeply shocked by behaviors that other Americans deemed normal, including working on Sundays and drinking. In contrast, they held the "Sabbath day" sacred and supported the temperance movement, which aimed to reduce or outlaw drinking. It's unlikely that their fire-and-brimstone preachers would have entertained supernatural tales about fairies.

Having said that, nothing in the history of belief is ever clear-cut: a few peripheral sources do suggest that Welsh immigrants may have indulged in

To this day, the town of Remsen continues to celebrate its roots by displaying the Welsh red dragon on flags and buildings. *Author's photo.*

storytelling about the Fair Folk. Significantly, one minister in Caernarfonshire (mentioned in the classic book *The Fairy-Faith in Celtic Countries*) actually encouraged his congregation to indulge in tales about fairies as a means of entertainment. This suggests that some non-Anglican ministers may have left the fairy faith of their parishioners intact. But what evidence do we have that such beliefs crossed the Atlantic and settled in these hills?

One story, which might represent a demonization of fairy belief, concerns a physician called Daniel Roberts who came to Steuben from Caernarfonshire in the early 1800s to set up a medical practice. Much loved by his fellow Welshmen, Dr. Roberts practiced an unorthodox type of medicine involving herbal concoctions and mesmerism. If rumors are to be believed, he also practiced a form of magic. The curious stories that have circled around Dr. Roberts are too numerous to mention here; the most relevant, for the purpose of this book, was told by his own brother:

One night at midnight, the doctor called his brother to the barn and drew a magic circle on the floor. After inviting his brother inside the circle, he read some words from a handy grimoire. According to historian Millard F.

Roberts (who heard the tale from a man who'd known the brother), what happened next was truly diabolical:

> *Immediately there came a sound as of falling hailstones upon the roof, and dark, shadowy objects appeared in the gloom all about them, though none ventured within the charmed circle where the two men stood. What mission the doctor dispatched these imps upon after summoning them to his presence, the brother failed to explain. Possibly he sent them to bail out his well with sieves, as was the case with one whom we have heard of, who, being a novice in the business, had acquired the art of calling spirits into his presence but not the power to dismiss them.*

Although the "imps" mentioned here appear to be associated with diabolical magic, it's possible they represent a Calvinistic demonization of fairy beings. Instead of resembling a fairy healer who used fairy-given powers to heal local people (as one might expect of a mystical Welsh healer or "cunning man"), Dr. Roberts is cast here as a type of wizard skilled in occult arts. Rather than learning his powers from the fairies, he summons "dark, shadowy" imps, apparently to serve him on an unnamed mission.

My question is: Does the portrayal of these imps (which appear to be minor demons rather than Fair Folk) imply a kind of folkloric transformation of Welsh fairy belief under the influence of Calvinism? British fairy folklore expert John Kruse has pointed out that when the word *imp* was first used in the British Isles (in the sixteenth century), it was interchangeable with the word *fairy*, suggesting that the two beings were one and the same thing. The Welsh word for elf—*ellyll*—also eventually came to refer to a type of hellish apparition, suggesting that Welsh elves may occasionally have been construed as imp-like beings. We might conclude from this that at some point in the sixteenth century, people began to call fairies *imps* under the influence of a Calvinistic theology that uniformly associated supernatural phenomena with the Devil. Over time, the shared nature of imps and fairies was forgotten, the former being construed as denizens of hell, the latter as residents of an ambiguous otherworld not easily conflated with either heaven or hell. It makes perfect sense, then, that the religious Welsh of Oneida County would have told tales about imps rather than fairies, unaware, perhaps, of their common origin.

While the story of Dr. Roberts's imps may not be conclusive evidence of early fairy stories among the Welsh of Oneida County, proof does exist from the twentieth century that immigrants brought some fairy stories with them from Wales. Folklorist Howard Thomas shared that in 1910, when he was twelve years old, he idolized a young Welshman called Hughey who'd recently arrived in Remsen from the Old Country. Hughey told the boy many tales about the *ellyllon* that, he said, haunted those who tended the lime kilns near his home.

Ellyllon were goblins or elves in Welsh folklore that sometimes performed helpful chores for farming households. Folklorist Wirt Sikes described them as "pygmy elves who haunt the groves and valleys, and correspond pretty closely with the English elves." If a group of ellyllon started performing tasks for a family late at night, they could be spied "working away like mad, and laughing and dancing as madly as they worked," but if they caught someone watching them, they soon scattered "like mist before the wind."

In the Welsh communities of Oneida County, the ellyllon evidently played amid the smoke that billowed from the lime-kiln furnaces while the limeburner was gazing into the fire. They may even have been attracted to the limestone itself, for in Welsh legends they eat "fairy butter," a type of fungus found deep within limestone crevices underground. Either that or they enjoyed the raucous atmosphere, for Remsen's lime kilns were social hotspots for the area's young men and boys, who liked to wrestle by the light of the fire. How well established these stories were in the villages of the Adirondack foothills is unclear, but one can easily imagine a limeburner, disoriented from the kiln's carbon monoxide fumes and the white-hot source of light, concluding that elves must be dancing in the smoke.

As for Howard Thomas, he clearly thought that belief in the ellyllon went back a long way among Remsen's Welsh immigrants: in 1964, he published *The Singing Hills*, a historical novel set in Remsen in 1845, in which he imagined the Welsh community talking in detail about the ellyllon. While most of the characters in the book are devout Methodists who don't put much stock in superstitious tales, other characters—more closely identified with old Welsh traditions—speak of the ellyllon in haunting terms. One character shudders when lightning flashes and wind shakes the house. "*Yr Ellyllon* are throwing stones in the hills," he says. He later describes the elves as "dancing around the room" in "green suits and little green caps." Another character called Pen Mari wanders the hills around Remsen lamenting the loss of her son Owen, whom she believes the ellyllon have stolen. When the ellyllon steal a child, they can keep him only for fourteen years, for after that, their power subsides. "Owen, little one," she cries, "the fourteen years are almost at an end. *Yr Ellyllon* can hold you no longer." We later learn that the woman, being an unwed

T.H. Thomas's depiction of a farmer meeting one of the ellyllon, as found in Wirt Sikes's *British Goblins* (1880). *Public domain.*

The Trenton Falls in Oneida County, legendary home of the Welsh "mist fairies," according to children's author James Parker. *Library of Congress.*

mother, had exposed the child on a hillside. She had since succumbed to the delusion that the ellyllon had "taken her baby." Elsewhere in the book, the ellyllon are called "goblins which inhabit our hills" and are said to steal "Welsh boys."

Besides stories about the ellyllon, whispers of other Welsh fairy stories do exist in the Adirondacks, although, regarding these, I've been unable to locate a substantiating source. The whispers I refer to are mentioned in a 2006 article in the *Boonville Herald*, a newspaper local to the western

Adirondack foothills. The journalist Judy Routson mentioned a legend brought to light by the artist and children's author James Parker, according to which fairies can be seen playing in the mists of the Trenton Falls "under the right conditions." According to the unsubstantiated legend, some of the early Welsh settlers who came to Trenton "claimed that they brought the fairies from Wales to America in wooden bird cages." When they arrived in Trenton, they released the fairies, which chose to live among the mists of the Trenton Falls, becoming "mist fairies."

Despite being labeled as "rooted in local legend," these fairy stories appear not to be based in traditional Welsh folklore, for fairies are never winged in old Welsh tales. It's possible the stories arose in response to an 1827 description of the Trenton Falls in the writings of John Sherman, a Unitarian minister. The first European to lay eyes on the falls and open them to public view, Sherman wrote that "at a certain hour of sunshine," a fairy "makes her appearance" in a huge excavation created by the water of the Sherman Falls (the first set of falls encountered at Trenton). She then "dances through the mist."

Rather than invoking a real-life fairy, Sherman was clearly describing a rainbow *personified* as a fairy, for the fairy "blushes" in every color as soon as she notices a visitor "gazing at her irised beauties." What we're dealing with here is clearly a fanciful use of language rather than a supernatural tale. It seems likely to me that the mist fairies of Trenton Falls owe their origin to Sherman's poetic devices rather than the Welsh fairy faith.

THE FAIRY CENSUSES

In the introduction to this book, I mentioned Twylah Nitsch and Jamie Sams's description of three different types of Little People who inhabit New York: the two-legged type that resemble humans, the winged type and the shining-light type. We've met many two-legged Little People in this book, originating in the traditions of various communities. Here, we'll meet the winged and shining-light types, for these are the most commonly seen Little People or fairies in New York today. We know this from the findings of the Fairy Censuses that academic Simon Young carried out between 2014–17 and 2017–23.

In those censuses, Young used an online survey to solicit descriptions of fairy experiences and beliefs from all over the world. In addition to asking generic questions such as the time of day when the encounter occurred, he also asked philosophical questions such as "What is a fairy?" The goal of the survey wasn't to gauge the prevalence of fairy beliefs in New York State but to discover the nature of the belief that does exist. While New Yorkers who believe in fairies are most likely a minority, this shouldn't lessen our interest in the censuses' findings, for a belief's rarity doesn't make it any less real. My goal in this section is to summarize the censuses' findings so we can better understand what New Yorkers believe about fairies today. Unfortunately, I'm not able to provide a location for any of these experiences, for the censuses withhold identifying information.

The Winged Fairy

Fairies have predominantly been depicted as tiny winged beings since the Victorian era, and this holds true for early twenty-first-century New York, where many people claim to have encountered this type of fairy. Closer to Tinker Bell than the fairies of old, winged fairies are no less real to the people who've encountered them than the fairies were to our ancestors.

The first example of a winged fairy is drawn from the experience of a twenty-something male respondent who woke one morning in spring to find that his bedroom was filled with a pink glow. At first, the man attributed the glow to some "dewy pink flowers" blooming in a tree outside his window. However, he soon became aware of a small being "skittering back and forth on the sill," looking out at the flowers. The being wore a cap and clothes made of dried leaves and had "long wings" that rose and fell in time with its breath. The being's skin was translucent like parchment, and beneath the skin, the man could see light. The man viewed fairies as nature spirits that protected the natural world and wished to enter into a creative relationship with human beings, especially in response to the current environmental crisis.

A similar experience of a pink winged fairy can be seen in one respondent's teenage memory of playing softball one afternoon. The girl was bored and not paying attention to the game when a tiny fairy (a "humanoid body with wings") flew past her, shimmering with a "pale rose" color. She said that the fairy was about the size of an "adult thumb" and didn't seem to be wearing any kind of clothing. Fairies, she said, are "mostly harmless," and the experience made her "very happy," but she also stated that fairies could be "annoying," such as "boggarts setting fire alarms off."

Illustrations such as this one by Warwick Goble (1920) appear to have played a large role in influencing contemporary beliefs about winged fairies. *Public domain.*

A common feature of winged-fairy encounters is childhood. The following three experiences all took place when the respondents were very young. The first respondent described being a young girl and seeing a fairy flying around her parents' dresser. The girl lived deep in the New York countryside, and both her parents were fast asleep. She described the fairy as being "female," having wings and possessing a small stature. She believed that fairies were "forest dwellers with some magical ability" and summarized the experience as a "fond vivid memory of my childhood."

The second respondent mentioned a memory in which he must have been about three or four years old. Although he'd always explained away the memory as the product of a fever dream (for he remembered the doctor making a house visit), he clearly recalled seeing a "winged fairy, probably three to four inches" in length, flying around his bed. In response to the question of whether fairies actually exist, the man admitted that he didn't know.

The final encounter from childhood concerned a girl who saw a fairy on two separate occasions. The first time, she was looking out through a glass door when she noticed a fairy with wings "like two leaves" and "dark eyes" stuck to the glass. The girl and the fairy maintained eye contact for a while before the fairy flew off. The second encounter occurred on a woodland trail, where the girl said she disturbed a fairy on a tree and watched it fly away; the fairy's wings were like leaves, and it was "vaguely humanoid," she said.

Each of these experiences can be categorized as a kind of beautiful, nonthreatening fairy encounter. This differentiates them, somewhat, from traditional fairy folklore in which the fairies are often threatening. We find a more dangerous type of winged fairy in the experience of a respondent who described being in the yard with her toddler daughter when the daughter began to giggle. When the mother looked over at the girl to see what she was laughing at, she saw tiny fairies surrounding the child and caressing her face and hair. The fairies resembled "dandelion fluff" and appeared to be luring the toddler away, for they were flying "towards her and then away and then back again." The mother "felt uneasy" and quickly brought the child inside. Here, we see the traditional folkloric motif of fairies attempting to steal young children, differing only in the fact that the fairies resembled "dandelion fluff," a rather nontraditional description.

The Shining-Light Fairy

No less commonly seen in New York than the winged fairy, the shining-light type of fairy is sometimes found in woodlands but can also be found in homes. Among the many woodland encounters is the story of a woman in her forties who was walking in the woods after midnight with one other person. The woman described "calling on" the fairies and watching as they started to "light up," manifesting in the form of "light and wings." A similar woodland encounter happened to a woman in her thirties who claimed to see an orb of orange light "moving around in the forest, leaving a trail." A few nights later, the woman saw several "bluish white" orbs emerging from a tree and flying as high as 150 feet in the air. The orbs hovered in the vicinity, "fading in and out" and "moving around quickly," for hours. The woman stated that fairies were "small, winged entities…able to travel in and out of their dimension and ours."

Although many of these experiences seem to confirm the commonly held belief that fairies are intrinsically associated with nature, a surprising number of New York encounters with shining-light fairies have actually occurred in people's homes. It seems that this type of fairy may be drawn to human habitations.

One example comes to us from a woman in her thirties who was lying awake in the dark next to her husband (who was sleeping) when she saw a "small ball of light" moving around the room. The light appeared curious, for it came close to her face and hovered there for a moment. While it remained in the same place, the woman saw a "human-like shape" inside the light, and then it disappeared. Significantly, the experience happened on Halloween, a night when the Fair Folk are known to roam abroad.

Other encounters with shining-light fairies from the censuses include the following: a young girl's sighting of a "ball of light" in the doorway of her home; a woman's sighting of a "rod of white light, about two inches long," bobbing in the corner of her room; and a young girl's description of waking up to a feeling of "intense energy" and "light orbs twinkling close to the wall and on the ceiling." Based on these encounters, it seems that the orbs seen in people's homes aren't noticeably different from those seen in woodlands; whether they're the same type of being is unclear.

Fairy Voices and Music

One particularly enchanting type of fairy encounter reported in New York is the experience of hearing fairy music and fairy voices. Although these encounters are quite rare, hearers have reported the sound of "chiming bells" or "glass bells tinkling" when no "churches" or "wind chimes" are within earshot. Other respondents have heard "tiny voices" speaking a language that isn't English. The sound may sometimes be extremely beautiful, as in the case of one man who described hearing a "multitude of very sweet, pleasing voices" while taking an excursion to see some fall foliage. In his case, the voices appeared to be "speaking the same words almost simultaneously, in a kind of cascading aural waterfall effect." When the man listened closely, he could make out what the fairies were saying; it was something along the lines of the following: "Don't you see us? We're all around you. Look—don't you see us?" Although the man had never taken an interest in fairies before, he was clearly shocked by the experience and came to believe that he'd heard the fairies' voices. He concluded that fairies were "spirits or spiritual beings of some kind, perhaps daemons."

Little People

Another rare New York fairy encounter is the sighting of Little People. While these fairies may have been the most frequently identified fairies in traditional folklore, Little People are found less often in present-day New York, especially compared to the more commonly seen winged fairies and shining-light fairies. Nevertheless, when Little People do appear to New Yorkers, they resemble traditional depictions of fairies quite closely.

One example of a Little People encounter in New York involves an animal-shape-shifting Little Person who approached some young men one night while they were busily drinking beer on a golf course. When the being approached, two of the men clearly described seeing a "little man." One of the men bent down, looked into the little man's eyes and determined that the being was about "eighteen inches in height." Quickly after this, the third friend exclaimed, "It's a skunk," and when the other two looked again, all they could see was a skunk. The little man then ran back the way he had come. The appearance of a fairy disguised as an animal appears to be quite a traditional description, for fairies often take animal forms in folklore.

Another Little People encounter happened to a woman one Halloween night after she'd been handing out candy to local children. The woman had a headache and went into the backyard to enjoy some fresh air. One corner of the yard had always seemed "off" to the woman, "overshadowed on three sides by tall trees," and nothing ever grew there. Now, she heard a rustling coming from the leaves piled up there, and when she looked in the direction of the sound, she saw "four or five little shadow figures." The woman described the figures as "miniature people about two-feet tall, but composed entirely of darkness." When she looked up, she saw more of them in the trees and on the roof of her garage, but these were "three-dimensional and moving around." The woman then ran back into the house and only returned later when they were gone. The woman has since developed a ritual of leaving wine and food for the Little People every Halloween night: on the morning of the first day of November, it's always gone.

One final Little People encounter involved a fourteen-year-old girl who came upon a tiny woman while walking in a woodland in Upstate New York. The girl had found two trees that were "wilting" over each other, forming the shape of a doorway. The girl heard a sound like a "giggle" and saw a small woman's silhouette at the base of the "doorway." The little woman appeared to be hiding from the girl, and the girl got scared, running back the way she had come. The girl later described fairies as "small mythical creatures with elemental powers."

A Fairy Procession

One of the most fascinating New York fairy sightings found in the censuses is that of a young girl who described looking out of her bedroom window in the small hours of the morning and witnessing what she called a "fairy processional"—that is, a long line of fairies processing down the street from a wooded area at one end of the street to a cemetery at the other. Fairy processions are found frequently in Irish and British folklore, where they're often associated with three special nights of the year when the fairies were thought to change their abodes (May Day Eve, Midsummer's Eve and Halloween); however, no sightings of fairy processions have ever been reported in New York folklore, as far as I'm aware.

The girl described the "processional" as a "column of fairies" wearing "white cloaks and carrying single candles in front of them." They appeared to be silent and wore their hoods up to hide their faces. The girl claimed that, in the moment, she didn't understand what she was seeing, but after doing some research, she concluded that it must have been a fairy procession. She described fairies as "ancient, magical folk that live in nature and sometimes have to move through the mortal plane."

A Spiritual Presence

Occasionally, rather than appearing in person, a fairy may reveal its presence to a New Yorker through feelings and sensations. This has occurred regularly to one female respondent in her fifties who claimed to have danced with the fairies many times without ever actually seeing them. She claimed that they communicated with her through "the wind and storm," and she always knew when they were there. When she felt sad and hurt, she said, she'd call on the fairies "automatically." She said the fairies were "non-human beings" and "magical creations."

As you can see, the fairies found in present-day New York are often very different from the ones found in folklore. Encounters with winged and shining-light fairies far outweigh encounters with the more traditional Little People. The development of this type of fairy encounter appears to owe its existence to Victorian conceptions of fairies, in which fairies were often depicted as beautiful young girls with butterfly-like wings. Before the Victorian era, fairies were rarely depicted in this light. Later, the influence of spiritual movements such as theosophy and the New Age contributed to an impression of fairies as beautiful, floating spirits and orbs of light. As a result, people in the modern age tend not to associate fairies with traditional characteristics such as crossroads dancing, fear of iron, abduction of children or the possession of physical bodies.

A GLOSSARY OF NEW YORK FAIRIES

BANSHEE

A female fairy who attaches herself to an old Irish family and wails when a member of that family is about to die. Described as a "good woman" by the Irish of New York City, she was depicted as wearing long white garments and floating in the air. She may have red hair and blue eyes, according to reports of the Blissville Banshee.

CHANGELING

A fairy placed with a human family after a human child has been snatched. Changeling cases have occurred in New York City and the towns of Port Leyden and Victor. An attempted changeling abduction occurred in Lisha's Kill north of Albany.

DEATH LIGHT

A dangerous, slow-moving yellow sphere or globe of light seen near Greece, a suburb of Rochester, usually when someone is about to die.

DJUGAT

Little People known to the Cayuga people. The male is called *degala* and the female *tcega'ha*.

DWARF
Seen outside the Van Rensselaer Mansion in Albany. Described as wearing a red hat and having a long white beard. Possibly a genius loci or guardian of the Van Rensselaer property. May also be synonymous with the Dutch kabouter or gnome.

ELLYLLON
Welsh elves or goblins that may have haunted the limeburners of Remsen, Oneida County, in the nineteenth and early twentieth centuries. They were believed to steal children.

EN-KWE-SHU-I-YEN
Little People whose name means "not men at all." Known to the Tuscarora people. About four feet tall. They wear fur caps and hunt with bows and arrows.

GAHONGA
Incredibly strong Little People known to uproot trees and throw boulders. When given tobacco, they shape rocks for the Haudenosaunee to use as axe-heads or grinders.

GANDAYAH
The friendliest tribe of Little People known to the Haudenosaunee. Called Drum Dancers because they're rarely seen but can be heard playing drums in the woods. They look after plants and seeds and paint the strawberries red in the summer. They hibernate in winter, sometimes under fallen leaves.

GNOMES
Little People who live in the Catskill Mountains and mine gold in an amphitheater of rock in Highmount. They brew a magical liquor that turned Henry Hudson and his crew into gnomes like themselves. In their gnome form, Hudson and his men appear in Highmount every twenty years in September.

GOBLINS
Little People found in the Hudson Highlands, particularly on Bannerman Island near Beacon. They control the winds and dance in the air. They dress in traditional Dutch garments. They only come out at night, for the sun may turn them to stone.

HEER OF DUNDERBERG
A goblin king or potentate that lives at the top of Dunderberg Mountain at the entrance to the Hudson Highlands. He oversees an army of goblins that control the weather, often sinking ships. He can be propitiated by tipping one's hat or lowering one's sails. He may be what the Dutch called a sea kobold.

HOBGOBLINS
A household spirit or domesticated goblin that lives near human settlements, including Old Fort Niagara and the Old Dutch Church in Kingston on the Hudson River.

IMPS
Small black beings summoned by the magical Welsh doctor Daniel Roberts in the town of Remsen in the southwest Adirondacks. Imps (sometimes called goblins) also serve under the Heer of Dunderberg. They may be the same beings as fairies or elves.

JUNGEOH
Little People who live in the three waterfalls of Letchworth State Park, known to the Seneca Nation. See the separate entries on the three tribes of Jungeoh: the Gahonga, the Ohdanwas and the Gandayah.

LITTLE PEOPLE
A term used for various types of fairy, including Irish fairies seen in the town of Greece, miniature beings found in the Adirondacks and the magical beings of Native American folklore found throughout the Finger Lakes and the Mohawk Valley.

MIST FAIRIES
Tiny winged fairies that play amid the mists of Trenton Falls in Oneida County. They supposedly arrived in America in wooden bird cages. Of Welsh origin.

NANI'TIS
Spirits that inhabit dolls among the Lenape People. Known as "doll beings," they are mainly owned by women. The spirit inhabiting the doll is called the "guardian of health" and is propitiated once a year in the fall with the Doll Dance ceremony.

OGWES'HA'I
Little People known to the Tuscarora people. About two feet tall, they speak in "whoops," wear "fine clothes" and hunt with slings.

OHDANWAS
Little People who live under water or in forests and plains underground. They protect the earth from giant snakes and the White Buffalo. They have pointy chins, froglike legs and large, webbed hands and feet.

SHINING-LIGHT FAIRIES
Small orbs of light of multiple colors seen throughout New York State. Occasionally found in woodlands, they're often drawn to human homes. The orb may enclose a human form with wings.

WEMATEGUNIS
Benevolent wood dwarves known to the Lenape people who lived on the island of Manhattan when the first Dutch immigrants arrived. The wood dwarves were believed to live in the forests and wetlands of present-day Manhattan and Queens. Between one and a half and three feet tall. They bestow great power and strength on those they meet. They usually appear at dawn or dusk. Sometimes they help lost hunters and are usually seen by small children.

WILL-O'-THE-WISP
A dangerous fairy light found in a swamp north of Herkimer. The fairy chases locals and has been known to kill those it reaches.

WINGED FAIRIES
Tiny humanoid beings with insectoid wings or wings that resemble leaves. Often seen by children in private homes.

WITTE WIEVEN
In Dutch folklore, these "white women" live in wild places, often underground, and sometimes steal humans. It's unclear if they are ghosts or fairies or whether they represent people who've been turned into fairies after they've died. Sometimes considered wise women and healers but also feared. One may have occupied the abandoned Van Rensselaer Mansion.

YAGODINYA YUYOCKS
Little People known to the Mohawk people. Their name means "they throw rocks." Synonymous with the Gahonga or Stone Throwers known to the Seneca.

SOURCES

Adams, Richard C. *Legends of the Delaware Indians and Picture Writing*. Syracuse University Press, 1997.

Bayly, Thomas Haynes. "Killarney (A Legend)." *Dublin Penny Journal* 1, no. 16 (1832): 121–22.

Beauchamp, William Martin. *Iroquois Folklore*. Dehler Press, 1922.

Bierhorst, John. *The Deetkatoo: Native American Stories About Little People*. HarperCollins, 1998.

———. *Mythologies of the Lenape: Guide and Text*. University of Arizona Press, 1995.

Connolly, William. "April 24, 1887." Unpublished diary in the possession of the Greece Historical Society.

Converse, Harriet Maxwell. *Myths and Legends of the New York State Iroquois*. University of the State of New York, 1908.

Cornplanter, Jesse. *Legends of the Longhouse*. J.B. Lippincott, 1938.

Corry, Emmett. "A Gathering of the Clans." *New York Irish History* 11 (1997): 27–31.

DeVeaux, Samuel. *The Traveller's Own Book to Saratoga Springs, Niagara Falls, and Canada*. Faxon & Read, 1843.

Gutman, Herbert G. "Work, Culture, and Society in Industrializing America, 1815–1919." *American Historical Review* 78, no. 3 (1973): 531–88.

Halpert, Herbert. "The Devil and the Fiddle." *Hoosier Folklore Bulletin* 2, no. 2 (1943): 39–43.

Harrington, Mark Raymond. *Religion and Ceremonies of the Lenape*. Heye Foundation, 1921.

Herzfeld, Elsa G. *Family Monographs: The History of Twenty-four Families Living in the Middle West Side of New York City*. James Kempster Printing Company, 1905.

Irving, Washington. *Rip Van Winkle*. Black Dome Press Corp., 1989.

———. "The Storm-Ship." In *Bracebridge Hall*, 288–310. R.F. Fenno & Company, 1900.

Jones, Louis C. "The Little People." *New York Folklore Quarterly* 18, no. 4 (1962): 243.

Journal of Nervous and Mental Diseases. "Hallucinated Lunatics at Large." 10 (1883): 317–19.

Kruk, Jonathan. *Legends and Lore of the Hudson Highlands*. The History Press, 2018.

Kruse, John. "Witches' Imps, Faery Familiars." British Fairies. August 17, 2022. britishfairies.wordpress.com/2022/08/17/witches-imps-faery-familiars.

Laskowski, Cornelius J. "Polish Tales of the Supernatural Collected in Albany, N.Y." *New York Folklore Quarterly* 10, no. 3 (1954): 165–75.

Legends and Poetry of the Hudson. P.S. Wynkoop and Son, 1868.

Linn, M.B. "Irish Immigrant Healing Magic in Nineteenth-Century New York City." *Historical Archaeology* 48, no. 3 (2014): 144–65.

McAnally, D.R. *Irish Wonders*. Houghton, Mifflin and Company, 1888.

McNamara, Robert F. *Mother of Sorrows, Rochester, New York: 1829–1979*. Custombook, Inc., 1979.

Meder, Theo. *The Flying Dutchman and Other Folktales from the Netherlands*. Libraries Unlimited, 2008.

Mitchel, Paula Ann. "Old Dutch Church a Symbol of Kingston's History." *Daily Freeman*, July 21, 2021. www.dailyfreeman.com/2013/12/28/old-dutch-church-a-symbol-of-kingstons-history.

New York Times. "The Banshee of Blissville." March 17, 1884.

———. "A Red-Haired, Blue-Eyed Ghost." March 10, 1884.

———. "A Remarkable Case of Hallucination." March 18, 1863.

Owain, Iago ap. "The Early Welsh Settlers of Steuben and Vicinity." *The Cambrian* 7 (1864): 334–35.

Panchyk, Richard. *Hidden History of Queens*. The History Press, 2018.

Parker, Arthur C. *Seneca Myths and Folk Tales*. Buffalo Historical Society, 1923.

———. *Skundy Wundy and Other Indian Tales*. George H. Doran Company, 1926.

Parker, James. *Mist Fairies and Leprechauns of the Adirondack Mountains*. North Country Books, 2002.

Paterson Evening News. "Legends of Paterson." October 27, 1900.

Powers, Mabel. *Stories the Iroquois Tell Their Children*. American Book Company, 1917.

Roberts, Millard F. *A Narrative History of Remsen, New York*. Published by the author, 1914.

Rodes, Sara Puryear. "Washington Irving's Use of Traditional Folklore." *New York Folklore Quarterly* 13, no. 1 (1957): 3–15.

Roth, John. *American Elves*. McFarland, 1997.

Routson, Judy. "Little People of the Adirondacks, According to Jim Parker." *Boonville Herald*, March 15, 2006.

Sams, Jamie, and Twylah Nitsch.

. HarperCollins, 1991.

Sherman, John. *A Description of Trenton Falls*. William H. Colyer, 1847.

Sikes, Wirt. *British Goblins*. Sampson Low, Marston, Searle and Rivington, 1880.

Singleton, Bob. "Grim Tales from Old LIC." QNS. November 21, 2011. qns.com/2011/11/grim-tales-from-old-lic.

Skinner, Charles M. *Myths and Legends of Our Own Land*. J.B. Lippincott Company, 1896.

Thomas, Howard. *Folklore of the Adirondack Foothills*. Prospect Books, 1958.

———. *The Singing Hills*. Prospect Books, 1964.

Thompson, Harold. *Body, Boots, and Britches*. J.B. Lippincott, 1940.

Thorpe, Benjamin. *Northern Mythology: North German and Netherlandish Popular Traditions and Superstitions*. Edward Lumley, 1852.

Townsend, Camilla, and Nicky Kay Michael. *On the Turtle's Back: Stories the Lenape Tell Their Grandchildren*. Rutgers University Press, 2023.

Wall, Steve. *Wisdom's Daughters: Conversations with Women Elders of Native America*. HarperCollins, 1993.

Waxman, Mitch. "The Blissville Banshee." The Brownstoner, October 10, 2013. www.brownstoner.com/history/the-blissville-banshee.

Werner, James. "The Old Dutch Church." JWWerner.com, February 2013. jwwerner.com/ODC/OldDutchChurch.html.

Winfield, Mason. "The Halloween Article: The Little People." Buffalo Rising, October 31, 2022. www.buffalorising.com/2022/10/the-halloween-article-the-little-people.

———. *Iroquois Supernatural*. Simon & Schuster, 2011.

Witthoft, John, and Wendell S. Hadlock. "Cherokee-Iroquois Little People." *Journal of American Folklore* 59, no. 234 (1946): 413–22.

Wonderley, Anthony. *Oneida Iroquois Folklore, Myth, and History*. Syracuse University Press, 2024.

Wozniak, Edward. "The Gnomes of the Catskills." Balladeer's Blog, October 3, 2015. glitternight.com/2015/10/03/the-gnomes-of-the-catskills.

Young, Simon. "The Fairy Census 2014–2017." The Fairyist, January 8, 2018. www.fairyist.com/wp-content/uploads/2014/10/The-Fairy-Census-2014-2017-1.pdf.

———. "The Fairy Census 2: 2017–2023." The Fairyist. www.fairyist.com/wp-content/uploads/2023/12/Fairy-Census2FINAL.pdf.

Young, Simon, and Chris Woodyard. "Three Notes and a Handlist of American Fairies." *Supernatural Studies* 6, no. 1 (2019): 56–85.

ABOUT THE AUTHOR

Andrew Warburton grew up in Bristol, England. He received his master's in creative writing at Bath Spa University and has published poems and short stories. He lived in Massachusetts for many years and now lives in Rhode Island. *New York Fairies* is the follow-up to *New England Fairies: A History of the Little People of the Hills and Forests*. He blogs about fairies at fairiesofnewengland.com.